MW01077994

Christmas Piano Songs

FOR DUMMIES®

Performance Notes by Bob Gulla

ISBN: 978-1-4234-2325-6

HAL•LEONARD®
CORPORATION

7777 W. BLUEMOUND RD. P.O. BOX 13819 MILWAUKEE, WI 53213

For all works contained herein:
Unauthorized copying, arranging, adapting, recording, or public performance is an infringement of copyright.
Infringers are liable under the law.

Visit Hal Leonard Online at
www.halleonard.com

Table of Contents

Introduction

••

*W*elcome to *Christmas Piano Songs For Dummies!* In this festive collection, you can find everything you need to play the latest and greatest holiday classics. I include as many standards as I could cram in here, with all the great piano and vocal arrangements you've come to expect. Though you may find some of the songs a bit challenging, be assured that a number of easier songs are included as well. In addition, I give you the kind of insightful performance notes that can help you play through these wonderful songs.

About This Book

The music in this book is in standard piano notation — a staff for the melody and lyrics above the traditional piano grand staff. Above the staff, you find the basic chords, along with guitar frames. I assume you know a little something about reading music, and that you know a little bit about playing piano (and possibly guitar) — such as how to hold your fingers, basic chords, and how to look cool while doing it. If you need a refresher course on piano, please check out *Piano For Dummies* by Blake Neely (Wiley).

How to Use This Book

For every song here, I include a little background or history. Sometimes I discuss the artist, the song's background, or some other, often trivial or otherwise interesting, element of the song. This information is followed by a variety of tidbits that struck me as I made my way through the teaching of these songs, including some of the following:

✔ A run-down of the parts you need to know.

✔ A breakdown of some of the chord progressions important to playing the song effectively.

✔ Some of the critical information you need to navigate the sheet music.

✔ Some tips and shortcuts you can use to expedite the learning process.

In many cases, you may already know how to do some of the things that I suggest. If so, please feel free to skip over those familiar bits.

I recommend that you first play through the song, and then practice all the main sections and chords. From there, you can add the tricks and treats of each one, and there are many, especially in these dandy holiday arrangements. Approach each song one section at a time and then assemble them together in a sequence. This technique helps to provide you with a greater understanding of how the song is structured, and enables you to play it through more quickly.

In order to follow the music and my performance notes, you need a basic understanding of scales and chords. But if you're not a wiz, don't worry. Just spend a little time with the nifty tome *Music Theory For Dummies* by Michael Pilhofer and Holly Day (Wiley), and with a little practice, you'll be on your way to entertaining family and friends at your next holiday gathering.

Glossary

As you might expect, I use quite a few musical terms in this book. Some of these may be unfamiliar to you, so here are a few right off the bat that can help your understanding of basic playing principles:

- ✔ **Arpeggio:** Playing the notes of a chord one at a time rather than all together
- ✔ **Bridge:** Part of the song that is different from the verse and the chorus, providing variety and connecting the other parts of the song to each other
- ✔ **Coda:** The section at the end of a song, which is sometimes labeled with the word "coda"
- ✔ **Chorus:** The part of the song that is the same each time through, usually the most familiar section
- ✔ **Chromatic:** Moving by half steps, as in the example of C–B–B♭–A–A♭–G
- ✔ **Hook:** A familiar, accessible, or singalong melody, lick, or other section of the song
- ✔ **Progression:** A series of chords played in succession
- ✔ **Resolution:** A type of progression that creates a sense of closure
- ✔ **Slash chord:** A chord with a specific bass note listed to the right of the chord name — C/G, for example
- ✔ **Suspended chord:** Also known as a sus chord: a chord where the 3rd has been raised to the 4th
- ✔ **Verse:** The part of the song that tells the story; each verse has different lyrics, and each song generally has between two and four of these

Icons Used in This Book

In the margins of this book are lots of little icons that will help make your life easier:

A reason to stop and review advice that can prevent personal injury to your fingers, your brain, or your ego.

Optional parts, or alternate approaches, that those who'd like to find their way through the song with a distinctive flair can take. Often these strategies are slightly more challenging routes, but encouraged nonetheless, because there's nothing like a good challenge!

Notes about specific musical concepts that are relevant but confusing to non-musical types — stuff that you wouldn't bring up, say, at a frat party or at your kid's soccer game.

You get lots of these tips, because the more playing suggestions I can offer, the better you'll play. And isn't that what it's all about?

Shortcuts and techniques that you can take that help, well, *save time.*

Auld Lang Syne

Words by Robert Burns
Traditional Scottish Melody

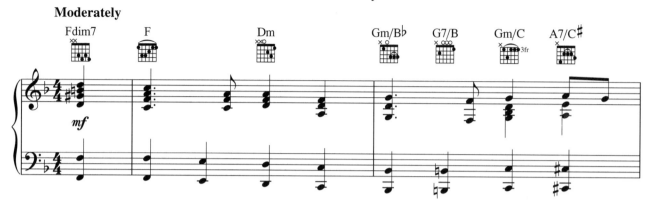

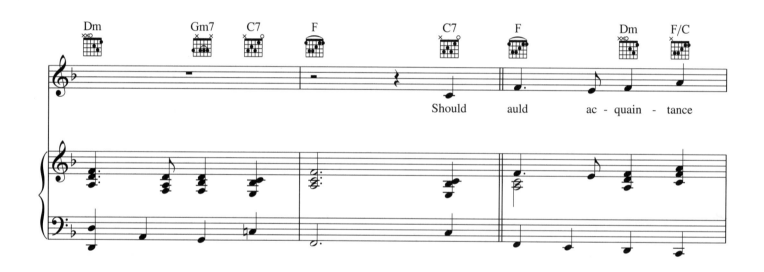

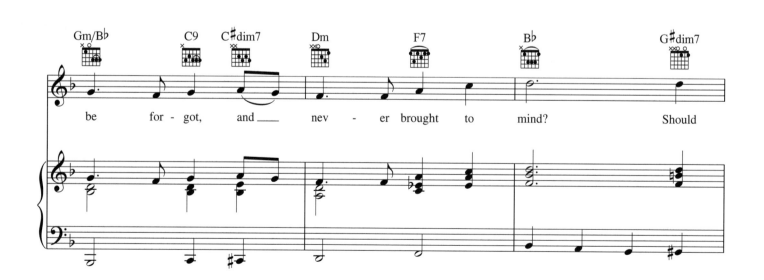

Copyright © 1982 by HAL LEONARD CORPORATION
International Copyright Secured   All Rights Reserved

Away in a Manger

Anonymous Text
Music by James R. Murray

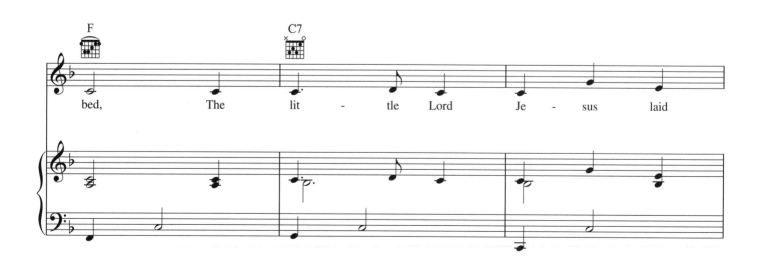

Copyright © 1993 by HAL LEONARD CORPORATION
International Copyright Secured   All Rights Reserved

Brazilian Sleigh Bells

By Percy Faith

Bright Samba

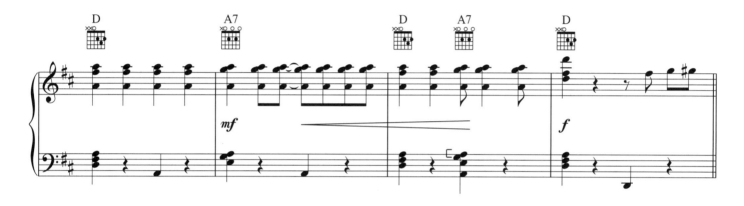

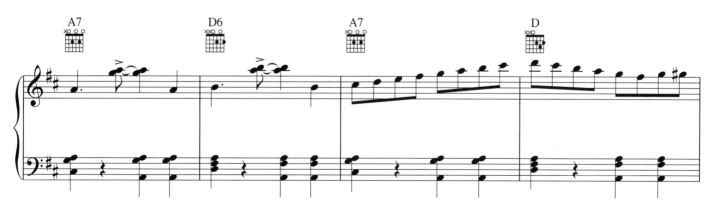

Copyright © 1950 UNIVERSAL - POLYGRAM INTERNATIONAL PUBLISHING, INC. and DROLET MUSIC
Copyright Renewed
All Rights Controlled and Administered by UNIVERSAL - POLYGRAM INTERNATIONAL PUBLISHING, INC.
All Rights Reserved   Used by Permission

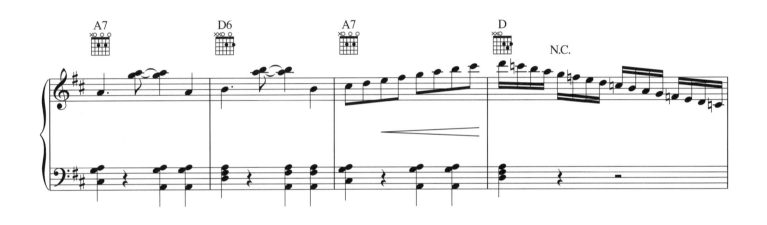

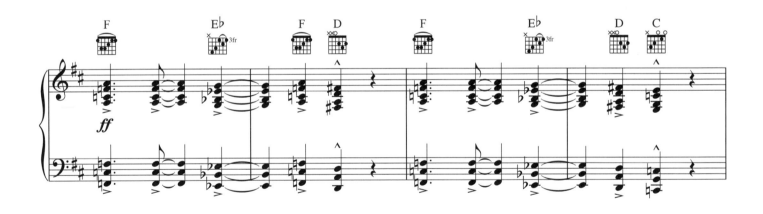

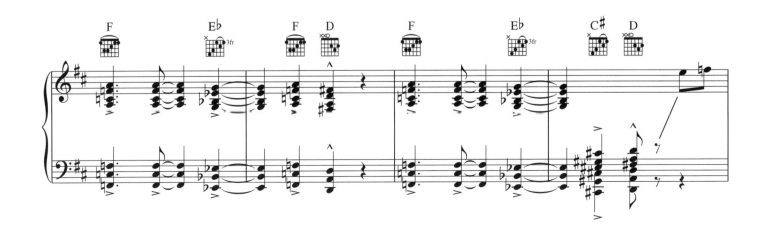

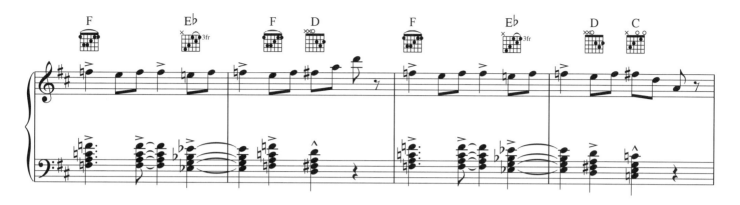

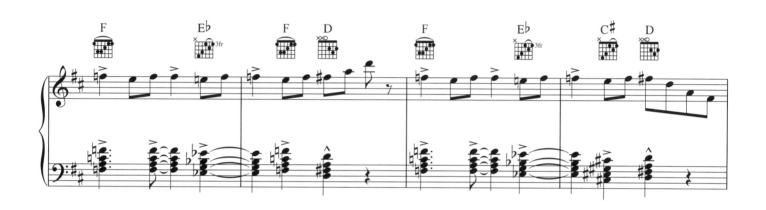

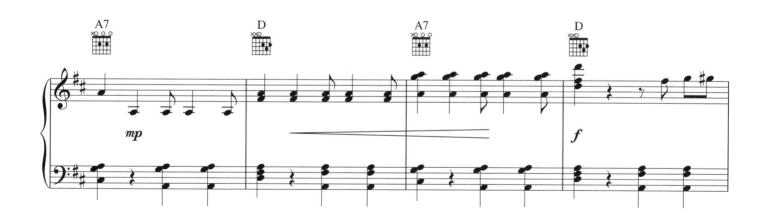

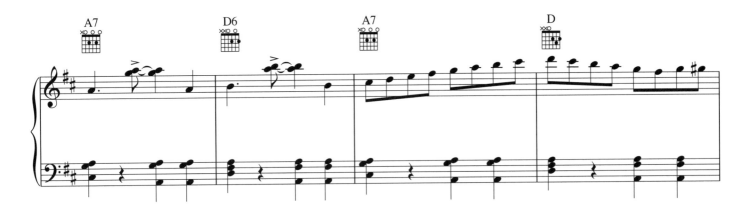

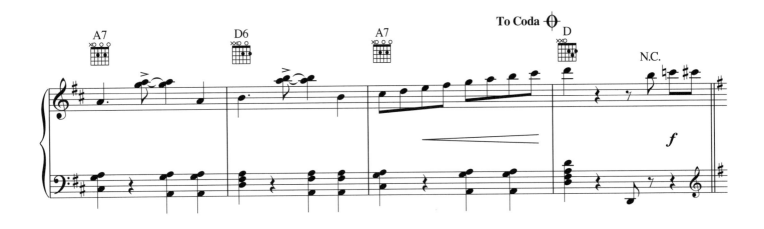

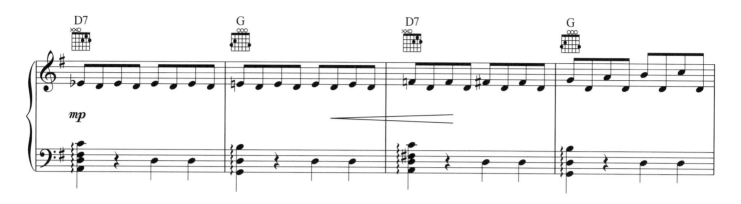

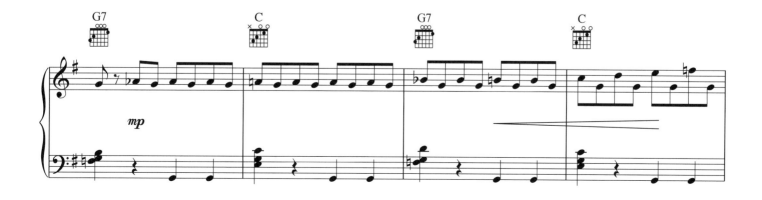

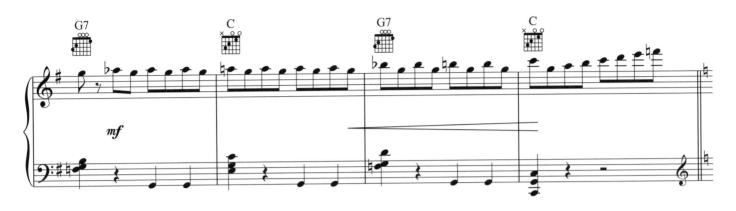

Blue Christmas

Words and Music by Billy Hayes and Jay Johnson

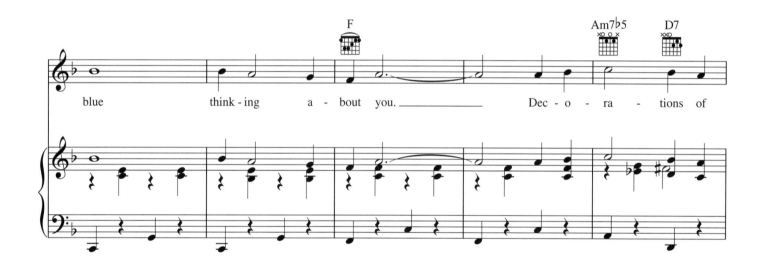

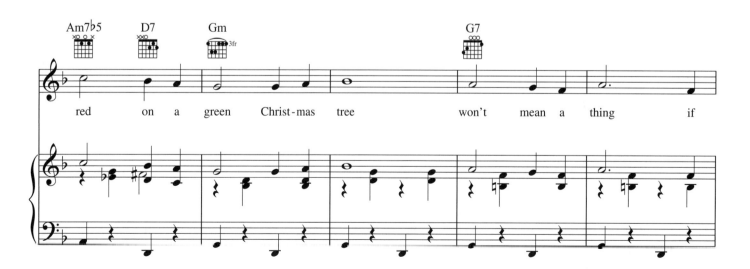

Copyright © 1948 UNIVERSAL - POLYGRAM INTERNATIONAL PUBLISHING, INC.
Copyright Renewed
All Rights Reserved   Used by Permission

The Chipmunk Song

Words and Music by Ross Bagdasarian

Copyright © 1958 Bagdasarian Productions LLC
Copyright Renewed
All Rights Reserved   Used by Permission

Christmas Is

Lyrics by Spence Maxwell
Music by Percy Faith

Christ-mas is sleigh - bells,　Christ-mas is shar - ing,

Christ-mas is hol - ly,　Christ-mas is car - ing.

Copyright © 1966 UNIVERSAL - POLYGRAM INTERNATIONAL PUBLISHING, INC.
Copyright Renewed
All Rights Reserved　Used by Permission

Christmas Is A-Comin' (May God Bless You)

Words and Music by Frank Luther

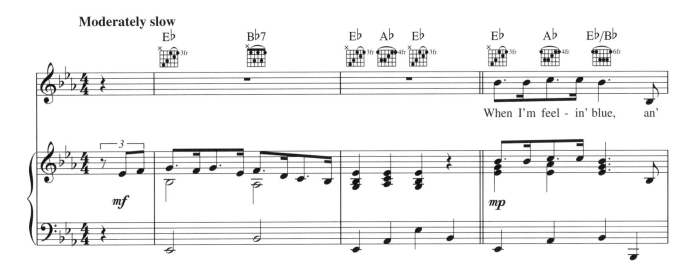

When I'm feel - in' blue, an'

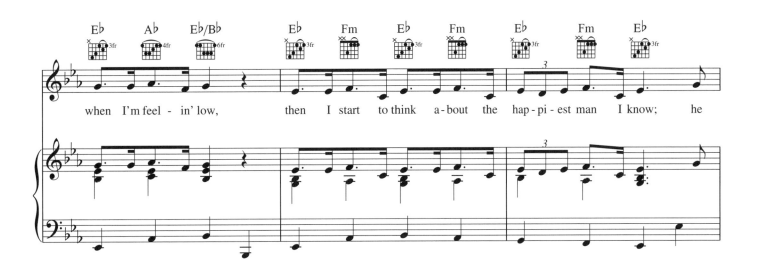

when I'm feel - in' low, then I start to think a - bout the hap - pi - est man I know; he

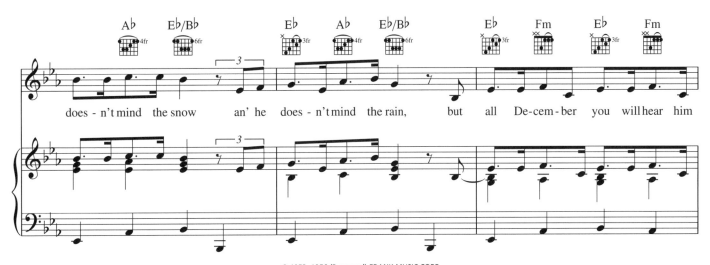

does - n't mind the snow an' he does - n't mind the rain, but all De - cem - ber you will hear him

© 1953, 1956 (Renewed) FRANK MUSIC CORP.
All Rights Reserved

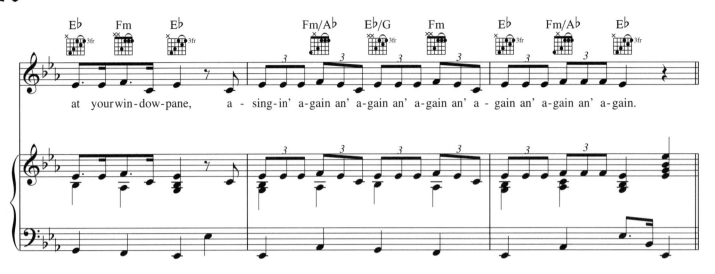

at your win-dow-pane,   a - sing-in' a-gain an' a-gain an' a-gain an' a - gain an' a-gain an' a-gain.

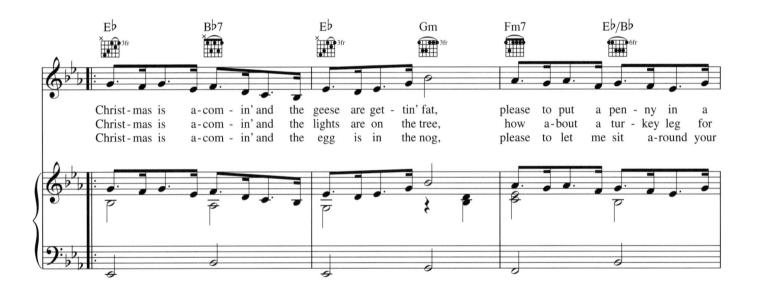

Christ-mas is   a-com - in' and   the   geese   are   get - tin' fat,   please   to   put   a   pen - ny   in   a
Christ-mas is   a-com - in' and   the   lights   are   on   the tree,   how   a-bout   a   tur - key leg   for
Christ-mas is   a-com - in' and   the   egg   is   in   the nog,   please   to   let   me   sit   a-round your

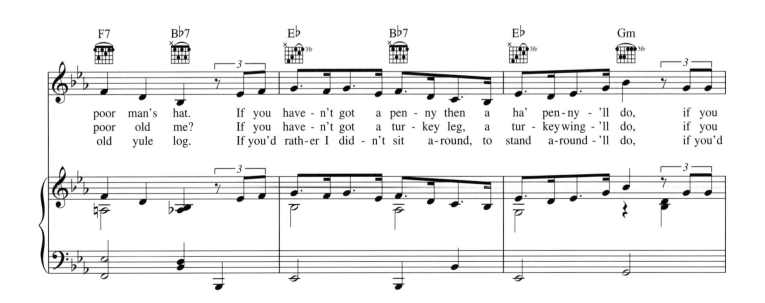

poor   man's   hat.   If   you   have - n't   got   a   pen - ny   then   a   ha' pen-ny - 'll do,   if you
poor   old   me?   If   you   have - n't   got   a   tur - key leg,   a   tur - key wing - 'll do,   if you
old   yule   log.   If   you'd   rath - er   I   did - n't   sit   a-round,   to   stand   a-round - 'll do,   if you'd

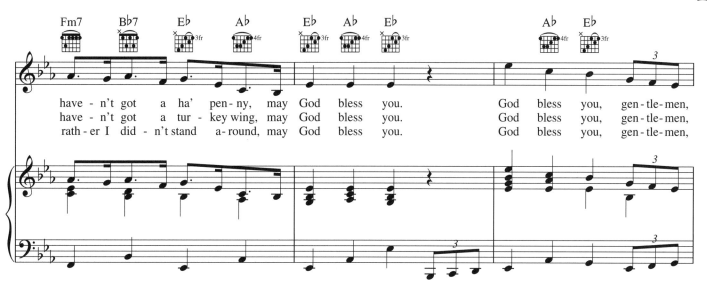

have - n't got a ha' pen - ny, may God bless you. God bless you, gen - tle - men,
have - n't got a tur - key wing, may God bless you. God bless you, gen - tle - men,
rath - er I did - n't stand a - round, may God bless you. God bless you, gen - tle - men,

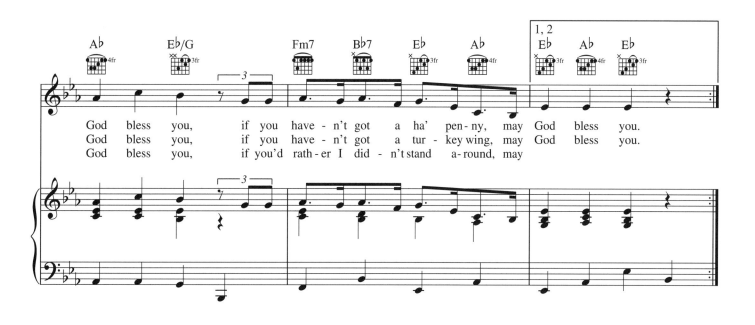

God bless you, if you have - n't got a ha' pen - ny, may God bless you.
God bless you, if you have - n't got a tur - key wing, may God bless you.
God bless you, if you'd rath - er I did - n't stand a - round, may

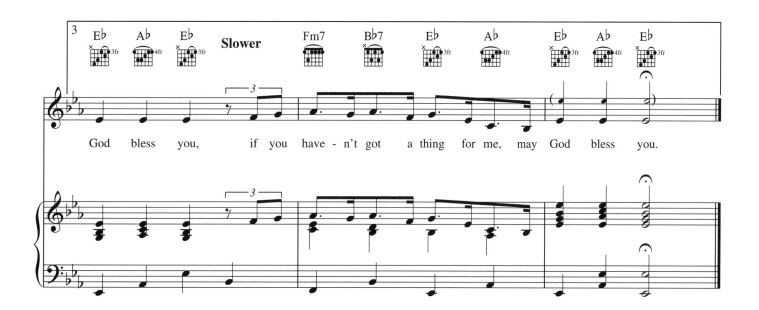

God bless you, if you have - n't got a thing for me, may God bless you.

The Christmas Song
(Chestnuts Roasting on an Open Fire)

Music and Lyric by Mel Torme and Robert Wells

© 1946 (Renewed) EDWIN H. MORRIS & COMPANY, A Division of MPL Music Publishing, Inc. and SONY/ATV MUSIC PUBLISHING LLC
All Rights on behalf of SONY/ATV MUSIC PUBLISHING LLC Administered by SONY/ATV MUSIC PUBLISHING LLC, 8 Music Square West, Nashville, TN 37203
All Rights Reserved

Christmas Time Is Here

from A CHARLIE BROWN CHRISTMAS
Words by Lee Mendelson
Music by Vince Guaraldi

Copyright © 1966 LEE MENDELSON FILM PRODUCTIONS, INC.
Copyright Renewed
International Copyright Secured   All Rights Reserved

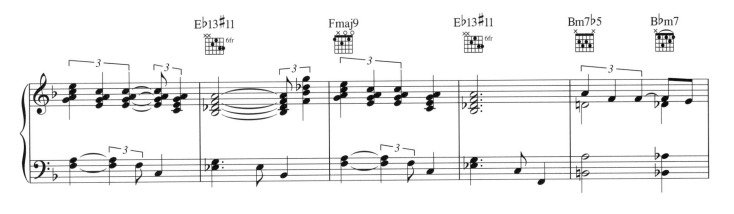

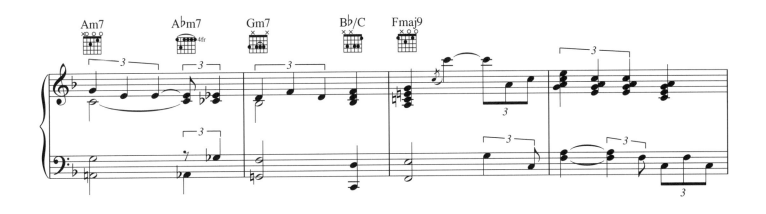

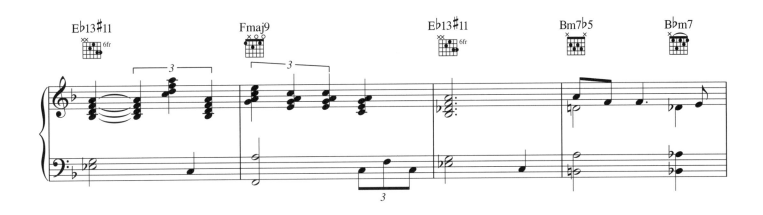

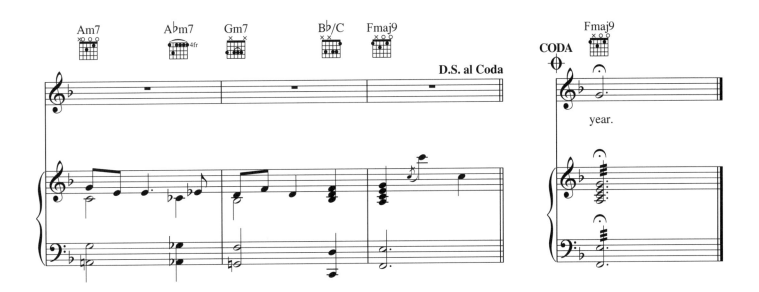

Deck the Hall

Traditional Welsh Carol

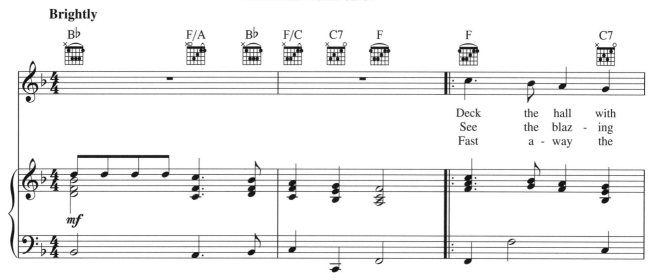

Deck   the hall   with
See   the blaz - ing
Fast   a - way   the

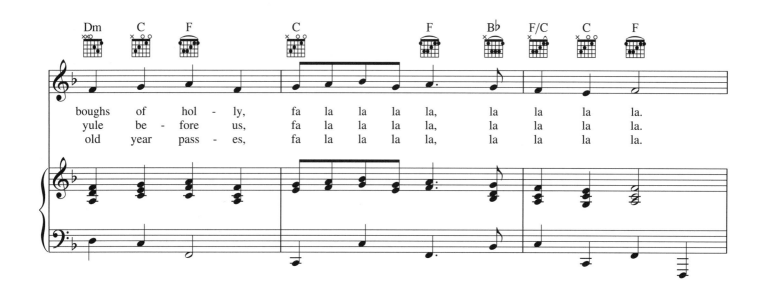

boughs   of   hol - ly,   fa   la   la   la   la,   la   la   la   la.
yule   be - fore   us,   fa   la   la   la   la,   la   la   la   la.
old   year   pass - es,   fa   la   la   la   la,   la   la   la   la.

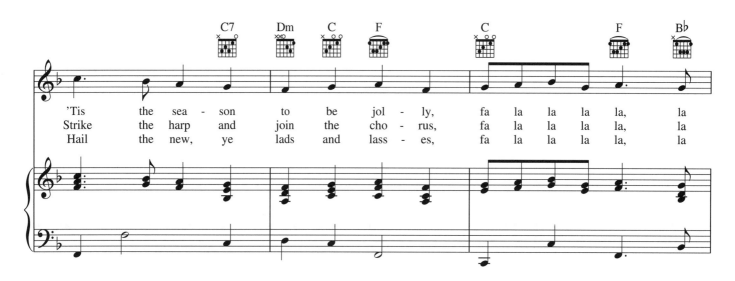

'Tis   the   sea - son   to   be   jol - ly,   fa   la   la   la   la,   la
Strike   the   harp   and   join   the   cho - rus,   fa   la   la   la   la,   la
Hail   the   new,   ye   lads   and   lass - es, fa   la   la   la   la,   la

Copyright © 2002 by HAL LEONARD CORPORATION
International Copyright Secured   All Rights Reserved

la la la. Don we now our gay ap - par - el,
la la la. Fol - low me in mer - ry meas - ure,
la la la. Sing we joy - ous all to - geth - er,

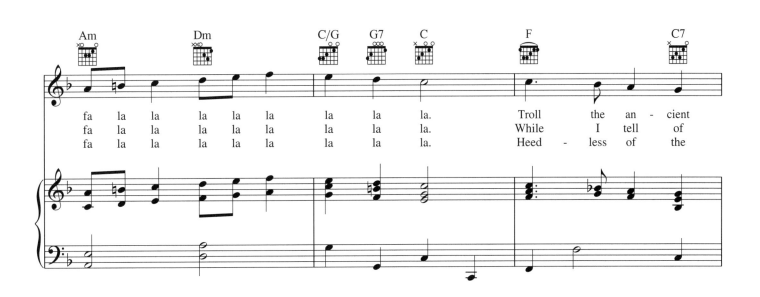

fa la la la la la la la la. Troll the an - cient
fa la la la la la la la la. While I tell of
fa la la la la la la la la. Heed - less of the

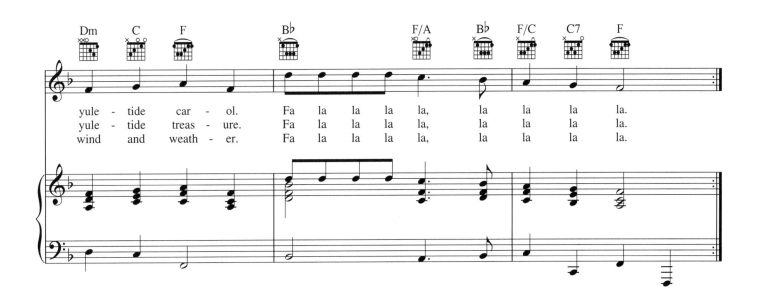

yule - tide car - ol. Fa la la la la, la la la la.
yule - tide treas - ure. Fa la la la la, la la la la.
wind and weath - er. Fa la la la la, la la la la.

Do You Hear What I Hear

Words and Music by Noel Regney and Gloria Shayne

Copyright © 1962 (Renewed) by Jewel Music Publishing Co., Inc. (ASCAP)
International Copyright Secured All Rights Reserved
Used by Permission

Feliz Navidad

Music and Lyrics by Josè Feliciano

Copyright © 1970 J & H Publishing Company (ASCAP)
Copyright Renewed
All Rights Administered by Stollman and Stollman o/b/o J & H Publishing Company
International Copyright Secured All Rights Reserved

The First Noel

17th Century English Carol
Music from W. Sandys' *Christmas Carols*

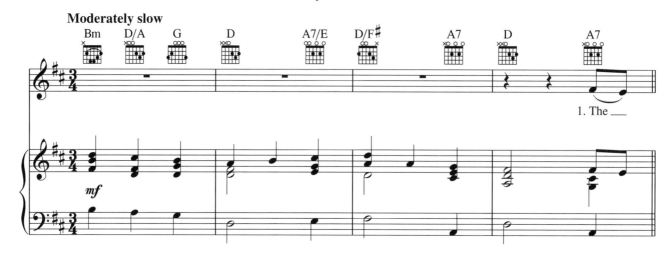

1. The __

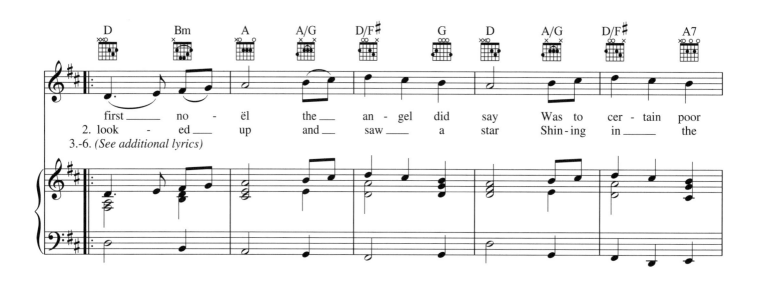

first __ no - ël the __ an - gel did say Was to cer - tain poor
2. look - ed __ up and __ saw __ a star Shin - ing in __ the
3.-6. *(See additional lyrics)*

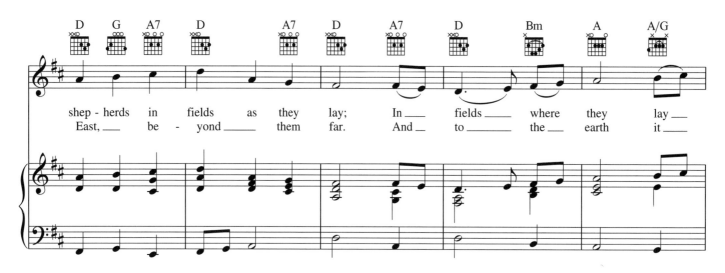

shep - herds in fields as they lay; In __ fields __ where they lay __
East, __ be - yond __ them far. And __ to __ the __ earth it __

Copyright © 1991 by HAL LEONARD CORPORATION
International Copyright Secured   All Rights Reserved

Additional Lyrics

3. And by the light of that same star,
   Three wise men came from country far.
   To seek for a King was their intent,
   And to follow the star wherever it went.
   Refrain

4. This star drew nigh to the northwest;
   O'er Bethlehem it took its rest.
   And there it did both stop and stay,
   Right over the place where Jesus lay.
   Refrain

5. Then entered in those wise men three,
   Full rev'rently upon their knee;
   And offered there in His presence,
   Their gold and myrrh and frankincense.
   Refrain

6. Then let us all with one accord
   Sing praises to our heav'nly Lord,
   That hath made heav'n and earth of naught,
   And with His blood mankind hath bought.
   Refrain

Frosty the Snow Man

Words and Music by Steve Nelson and Jack Rollins

Copyright © 1950 by Chappell & Co.
Copyright Renewed
International Copyright Secured   All Rights Reserved

Happy Holiday

from the Motion Picture Irving Berlin's HOLIDAY INN
Words and Music by Irving Berlin

© Copyright 1941, 1942 by Irving Berlin
Copyright Renewed
International Copyright Secured   All Rights Reserved

God Rest Ye Merry, Gentlemen

19th Century English Carol

Copyright © 1991 by HAL LEONARD CORPORATION
International Copyright Secured   All Rights Reserved

Grandma Got Run Over by a Reindeer

Words and Music by Randy Brooks

Copyright © 1984 by Kris Publishing (SESAC) and Elmo Publishing (SESAC)
Admin. by ICG
All Rights Reserved   Used by Permission

You can say there's no such thing as San - ta, but as for me and Grand-pa, we be -

lieve. ____

Additional Lyrics

2. Now we're all so proud of Grandpa,
   He's been taking this so well.
   See him in there watching football,
   Drinking beer and playing cards with Cousin Mel.
   It's not Christmas without Grandma.
   All the family's dressed in black,
   And we just can't help but wonder:
   Should we open up her gifts or send them back?
   Chorus

3. Now the goose is on the table,
   And the pudding made of fig,
   And the blue and silver candles,
   That would just have matched the hair in Grandma's wig.
   I've warned all my friends and neighbors,
   Better watch out for yourselves.
   They should never give a license
   To a man who drives a sleigh and plays with elves.
   Chorus

Happy Christmas, Little Friend

Lyrics by Oscar Hammerstein II
Music by Richard Rodgers

Copyright © 1952 by The Rodgers & Hammerstein Foundation
Copyright Renewed
WILLIAMSON MUSIC owner of publication and allied rights throughout the world
International Copyright Secured   All Rights Reserved

Happy Xmas (War Is Over)

Words and Music by John Lennon and Yoko Ono

So this is X - mas, and what have you
X - mas, and what have we

done? An - oth - er year o - ver, a new one just be -
done? An - oth - er year o - ver, a new one just be -

gun. _____ And so this is X - mas; I hope you have
gun. _____ And so hap - py X - mas; we hope you have

© 1971 (Renewed 1999) LENONO.MUSIC and ONO MUSIC
All Rights Controlled and Administered by EMI BLACKWOOD MUSIC INC.
All Rights Reserved   International Copyright Secured   Used by Permission

Hard Candy Christmas

from THE BEST LITTLE WHOREHOUSE IN TEXAS

Words and Music by Carol Hall

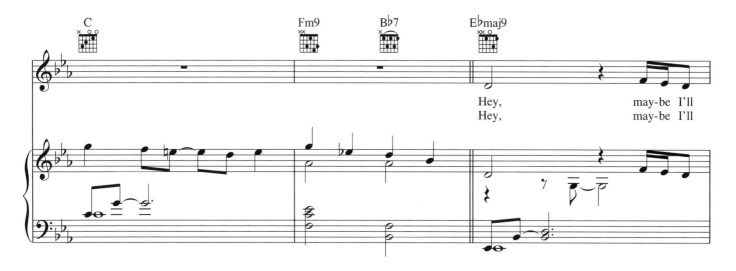

Hey,   may-be I'll
Hey,   may-be I'll

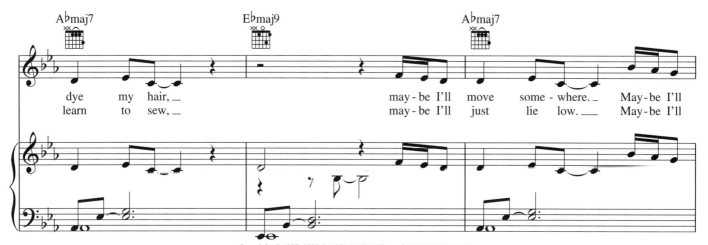

dye   my hair, __   may-be I'll move some - where. __ May-be I'll
learn to sew, __   may-be I'll just lie low. __ May-be I'll

Copyright © 1977, 1978 DANIEL MUSIC LTD. and OTAY MUSIC CORP.
Copyright Renewed
All Rights for the United States and Canada Controlled and Administered by UNIVERSAL MUSIC CORP.
All Rights Reserved Used by Permission

Hark! The Herald Angels Sing

Words by Charles Wesley
Music by Felix Mendelssohn-Bartholdy

Copyright © 2003 by HAL LEONARD CORPORATION
International Copyright Secured   All Rights Reserved

Here Comes Santa Claus
(Right Down Santa Claus Lane)

Words and Music by Gene Autry and Oakley Haldeman

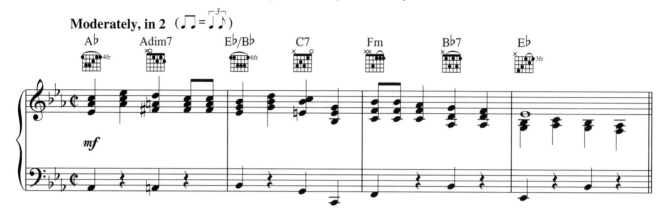

Here comes San - ta Claus! Here comes San - ta Claus! Right down San - ta Claus Lane!

Vix - en and Blitz - en and all his rein - deer are pull - ing on the rein.
He's got a bag that is filled with toys for the boys and girls a - gain.
He does - n't care if you're rich or poor, for he loves you just the same.
He'll come a - round when the chimes ring out; then it's Christ - mas morn a - gain.

© 1947 (Renewed) Gene Autry's Western Music Publishing Co.
All Rights Reserved   Used by Permission

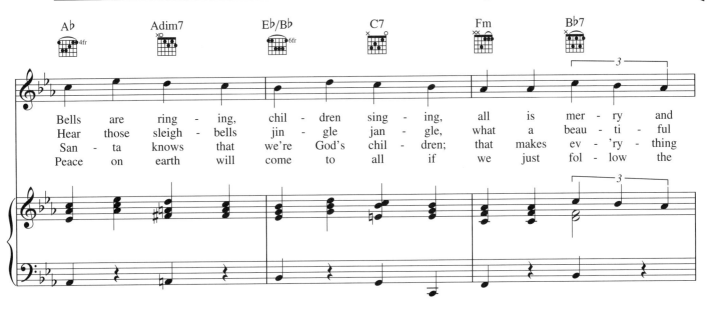

Bells are ring - ing, chil - dren sing - ing, all is mer - ry and
Hear those sleigh - bells jin - gle jan - gle, what a beau - ti - ful
San - ta knows that we're God's chil - dren; that makes ev - 'ry - thing
Peace on earth will come to all if we just fol - low the

bright. Hang your stock - ings and say your pray'rs, ⎫
sight. Jump in bed, cov - er up your head, ⎬ 'cause
right. Fill your hearts with a Christ - mas cheer, ⎪
light. Let's give thanks to the Lord a - bove, ⎭

1-3
San - ta Claus comes to - night.

4
San - ta Claus comes to - night.

A Holly Jolly Christmas

Music and Lyrics by Johnny Marks

Copyright © 1962, 1964 (Renewed 1990, 1992) St. Nicholas Music Inc., 1619 Broadway, New York, New York 10019
All Rights Reserved

(There's No Place Like) Home for the Holidays

Words by Al Stillman
Music by Robert Allen

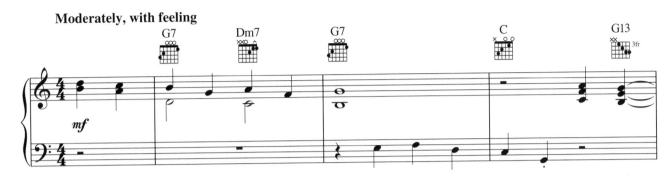

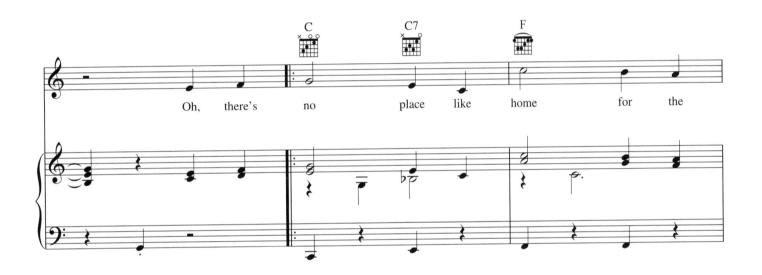

Oh, there's no place like home for the

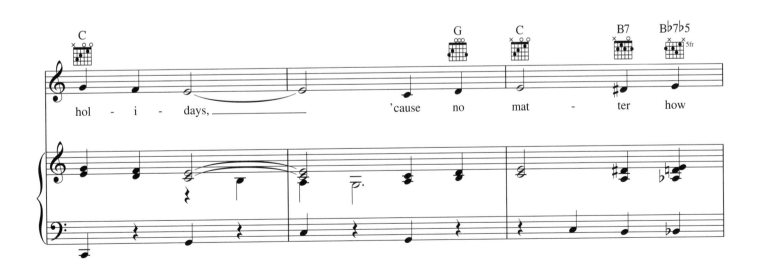

hol - i - days, _____ 'cause no mat - ter how

© Copyright 1954 Roncom Music Co.
Copyright Renewed 1982 and Assigned to Charlie Deitcher Productions, Inc. and Kitty Anne Music Co.
International Copyright Secured   All Rights Reserved

I Heard the Bells on Christmas Day

Words by Henry Wadsworth Longfellow
Adapted by Johnny Marks
Music by Johnny Marks

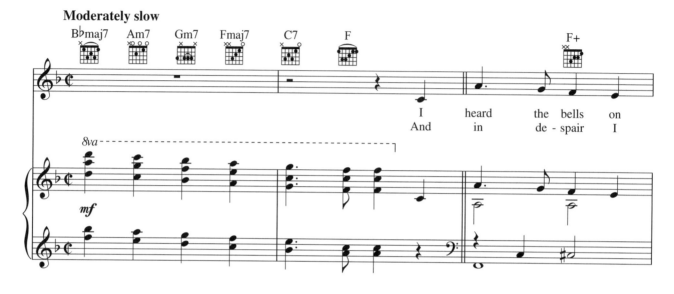

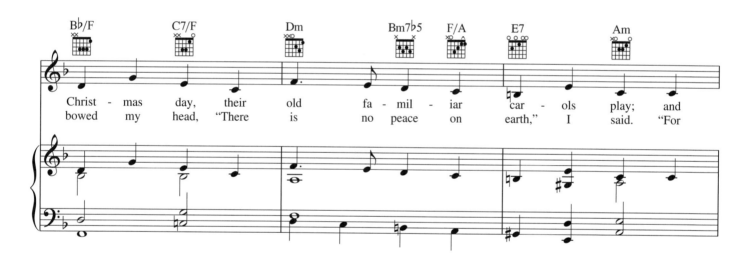

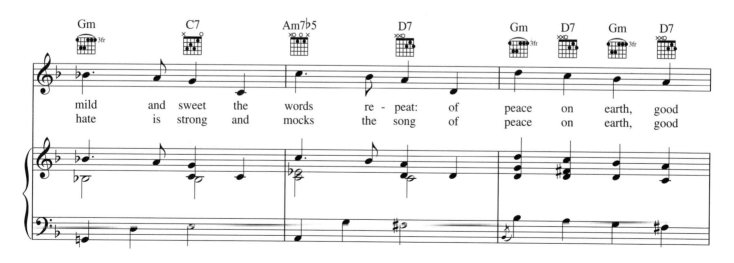

Copyright © 1956 (Renewed 1984) St. Nicholas Music Inc., 1619 Broadway, New York, New York 10019
All Rights Reserved

I Saw Mommy Kissing Santa Claus

Words and Music by Tommie Connor

Copyright © 1952 by Regent Music Corporation (BMI)
Copyright Renewed by Jewel Music Publishing Co., Inc. (ASCAP)
International Copyright Secured   All Rights Reserved
Used by Permission

I'll Be Home for Christmas

Words and Music by Kim Gannon and Walter Kent

© Copyright 1943 by Gannon & Kent Music Co., Inc., Beverly Hills, CA
Copyright Renewed
International Copyright Secured   All Rights Reserved

It Came Upon the Midnight Clear

Words by Edmund Hamilton Sears
Music by Richard Storrs Willis

Copyright © 1991 by HAL LEONARD CORPORATION
International Copyright Secured   All Rights Reserved

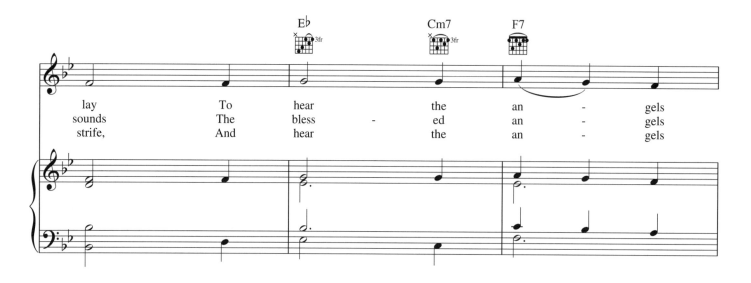

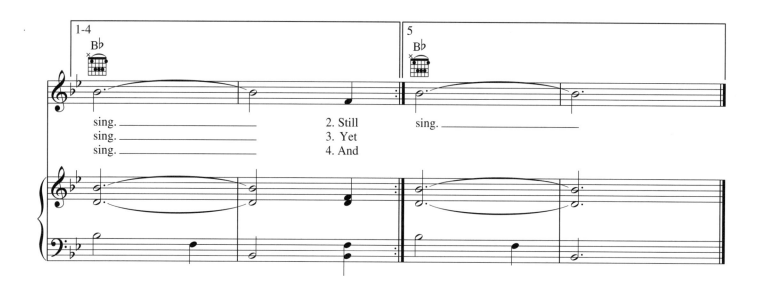

Additional Lyrics

4. And ye, beneath life's crushing load,
   Whose forms are bending low,
   Who toil along the climbing way
   With painful steps and slow,
   Look now! for glad and golden hours
   Come swiftly on the wing.
   O rest beside the weary road,
   And hear the angels sing.

5. For lo! the days are hast'ning on,
   By prophet-bards foretold.
   When, with the ever-circling years,
   Shall come the Age of Gold,
   When peace shall over all the earth
   Its heav'nly splendors fling,
   And all the world give back the song
   Which now the angels sing.

It's Beginning to Look Like Christmas

By Meredith Willson

© 1951 PLYMOUTH MUSIC CO., INC.
© Renewed 1979 FRANK MUSIC CORP. and MEREDITH WILLSON MUSIC
All Rights Reserved

Performance Notes

Auld Lang Syne (page 6)

"Should auld acquaintance be forgot?" I guess it depends on whether or not they owe you money! This old Scottish folk song about remembering times gone by has become one of the most popular songs the world has ever known. Its origins are murky. Robert Burns is commonly credited with penning the lyrics; however, in a letter that he wrote to a friend in 1788 he enclosed some of the lyrics, stating that they had thrilled him ever since he first heard them. This would seem to indicate that Burns later added a couple of his own verses to the existing lyrics, and then paired it with a traditional Scottish *air,* or melody, to create what is now recognized as "Auld Lang Syne." This nice little arrangement includes sweet passing chords to tug heart strings on New Year's Eve. Or anytime.

 Here's a practice strategy. Start by practicing the first verse first (where the singing starts). It's the easiest part. Then try the second verse (a little harder). Finally, go back and practice the introduction. Your fingers will be all warmed up by then.

 Don't be scared by the descending octaves in the introduction. The rest of the song uses single notes for the left hand bass. How to start? Practice right hand and left hand *separately* on the intro and combine them later. Still think it's too hard? Just play single notes instead of octaves. Add them later. I won't tell anyone. I promise!

The tight melodic range of the vocal makes this a wonderful singalong! Tenors, basses, sopranos, and altos can all hit these notes so no one is left out on New Year's Eve. Even if you don't get a kiss at midnight you can still sing your heart out. Also, go to the good old Internet (or your library) to find many beautiful extra verses to sing. The song structure basically consists of a four-bar intro, an eight-bar verse, and an eight-bar chorus. Notice that chorus and verse are eerily similar. If you sing extra verses, don't repeat the introduction.

Away in a Manger (page 8)

Contrary to popular legend, "Away in a Manger" was *not* written by Martin Luther, founder of the Lutheran church. The traditional Christian hymn was, however, originally published in a Lutheran Sunday School book, in 1885, with the subtitle "Luther's Cradle Hymn," which is likely what led to the confusion. The hymn, which is often one of the first Christmas carols taught to school children, actually has two melodies. One, "Cradle Song," is more typically heard in the United Kingdom. The other, which is the one presented here, is "Mueller," which was written by James R. Murray. If the tune in this book doesn't sound like the one you know, odds are you heard the other one in your cradle.

The four-bar intro to "Away in a Manger" contains essentially the melody and chords as the final four bars of each 16-bar verse. This is a very common way to begin a song, particularly in church-based arrangements.

Notice how the entire melody stays within one octave starting on middle C. This range indicates a good singalong. The key is not C, though. It's in F, so make sure to flat that B. And keep it mellow. It's a waltzy lullaby, not a rock 'n' roller.

 Check out the time signature on this one: 3/4. Waltzy, right? Sure, but later . . . Holy moly! The bass line has changed. Those eighth notes are rolling along. No wonder the baby awakes! Even the cattle probably interrupt their lowing. Six eighth notes per measure replace quarter and half notes. The time signature stays 3/4 but the feeling is 6/8. Stay calm. Don't accent that beat too much. It's not the famous Charlie Brown song, but a nice change that continues to the end.

Try the second half of the song first to make sure you have the chops to play the whole arrangement (or if you should even try when you're tipsy on eggnog at the holiday party). In any case, have fun!

Blue Christmas (page 18)

Elvis Presley effectively made this heartbroken ode to a lost holiday his own by imposing his trademark sad snarl on it for his 1957 classic recording. Prior to Elvis's cover, the Billy Hayes/Jay W. Johnson composition was a country music staple, covered by Ernest Tubbs and Chet Atkins. Since Elvis's cover, hundreds of rock and pop artists have taken a shot at it, from Brenda Lee and Celine Dion to Bright Eyes and Billy Idol, whose snarl is reminiscent of the King's! Guess there's something about white Christmases that just make folks blue! Now a Christmas classic, this song gets finer with age.

 Help! There's no intro! The first note is a sung melody. What if you want to sing the song or have someone sing along as you play? How can you find the starting pitch? Well, you could play *that* note on the piano. Awkward! Or use an accompanist's trick: Start the song with the *last* few (about eight) measures of the song — starting with "you'll be doin' all right . . . " Then just channel Elvis, baby.

 Practice the chromatic changes first. To find the chromatic changes, look at the guitar chords above the music. See how in some measures they change quickly (two per measure)? Holy Stravinsky, Batman! That's it.

Note the counterpoint between melody and accompaniment. The piano plays a straight 4/4 with bass notes on first and third beats. The melody, conversely, accents the second beat with sweet half notes. Elvis knew how to energize ballads like this, perfecting that rocking sensation over even oompah-esque, "could be a polka" beats. Well, the blues guys did it before him. And others, too, I'm sure.

Brazilian Sleigh Bells (page 11)

Percy Faith's beautifully arranged holiday music has become a fixture for many during the season. In most of his holiday work, Faith arranged classic compositions, featuring lush strings and a jubilant full choir of voices. But rather than go for obvious arrangements and cloying melodies, Faith focused on giving his listeners a little bit more, as he does here on the Latin-influenced handful (for a pianist), "Brazilian Sleigh Bells." This unpredictable tune can add variety to your Christmas repertoire if you've the chops.

 Start out slowly if need be: A lot is going on in this song. Look at the time signature. The c with a line through it signifies cut time — a 4/4 that's faster, so it becomes 2/2. This happens when quick, rhythmic songs use lots of quarter notes. This song uses a bright samba beat with dynamic markings galore so pay close attention. Also watch for arrows above accented notes.

 Coda alert! A couple of codas may have you bouncing around the song like a dancing bear. Codas are repeats that don't go back to beginnings of songs, but to other wonderful places. To navigate these codas, use a marker to highlight the coda markings so that you can quickly find your way around without straining your eyes.

Watch for the two treble clefs about halfway through the song, followed quickly by an *8va* (octave jump). Also, note the key changes from D to G to C and then back again. So roll up your sleeves, Beethoven. This is some real piano. Memorize it and watch the crowds dance all night long. A little extra effort and you'll really impress your listeners with this hot number.

The Chipmunk Song (page 20)

Christmas music has brought not only reindeer and barking dogs into our music repertoire, but squeaky-voiced Chipmunks as well. And if that's not strange enough, the song is the only Christmas recording to reach #1 on the *Billboard* Hot 100 pop chart, doing so in 1958. This composition by Ross Bagdasarian, Jr. entered the pop charts three times after that, in 1959, 1960, and 1962, and has sold nearly 5 million copies over the years. Not bad for a bunch of disobedient rodents.

Key alert: A♭! Run up and down the scale a few times to cement those four flats into your head.

If you're a guitarist (or jazz pianist) following the guitar chords above the music, make sure to practice this song before performance. The melody has some unexpected twists and turns (chromatics and passing tones) that affect voicing and timing on your chords.

Besides being sung by furry animals, this folky song in triple time contains unexpected intervals called *seconds* — notes within a chord, minor or major, that are a half or whole step apart. (For example, the first two notes of "Chop Sticks" are a whole step apart — major second). In the second measure of the introduction, look at the D treble note against the E♭ bass. Play them together. Hear that minor second? Sound odd or wrong? Well, it's not. (It sounds wrong just because, for a while, Western European composers didn't like it. So, our ears got brainwashed. But they got over it.) So forge on. You too will soon love these intriguing harmonies!

Christmas Is (page 22)

Percy Faith's highly recommended *Christmas Is* album was one of the '60s most popular and enduring holiday releases and a fixture in easy listening homes in the '60s and early '70s. The album included this song of the same name along with ten other holiday chestnuts. Faith, who arranged classics more frequently than he wrote them, produced the kind of quality material right alongside blockbuster names like Henry Mancini and Andy Williams. At a time when the pop charts were featuring more and more Motown and Beatles each passing year, Faith remained steadfast in his classy, instrumental elegance.

Although the time signature is 4/4, this tune uses lots of triplets. That number 3 you see above or below notes indicates three beats contained within one beat. It creates rhythmic variety without changing the overall structure or feeling of the song.

Keep the tempo moderate. The ascending melody may encourage you to speed up. This arrangement, however, replicates an orchestral feel where a conductor would be presiding over sweet strings and horns, swaying with a steady baton. This would be a nice calming piece after "Jingle-Bell Rock."

Portions of this song use two treble clefs so you may want to use a highlighting pen or pencil on those sections (but only if you *own* this book rather than borrowing it from your very particular brother or sister).

Use voicing to accentuate the actual sung melody. Play the melody a little louder so that it does not get lost in all the flowing accompaniment. Notice that the first triplet of almost every measure is either held or repeated. Don't forget, or you'll have an abrupt silence there which could "harsh the mellow" of this pretty tune.

Christmas Is A-Comin' (May God Bless You) (page 25)

Composed in 1953 by Frank Luther, this tune was made famous by Bing Crosby, the holiday season's warmest and most avuncular voice. Bing popularized this tune, along with songs like "The First Snowfall" and "Is Christmas Only a Tree," on his radio broadcasts before they were issued as singles in 1955. The song is an adaptation of a nursery rhyme, one frequently sung as a round: "Christmas is a coming, the goose is getting fat/Please put a penny in the old man's hat." In Luther's version, the song is similar: "Christmas is a coming, and the egg is in the nog. Please to let me sit around your old yule log." Pianists, a cappella choirs, and bluegrass artists alike love this simple, feel-good singalong.

This song uses lots of dotted eighth notes beamed to sixteenth notes. These snappy rhythmic figures are often called *dotted rhythms*. The vocal patter uses lots of dotted rhythms to move the story along. These dotted eighth-sixteenth figures are combined with a few triplets, scattered about, to further animate the plea of this hopeful vagabond.

Although one singer sings it, this piece has two distinctive vocal parts: the introduction and the song. The introductory verse is voiced by a narrator and the latter verses are voiced by the character, a cheery busker. You may want to reflect this in the tone of the playing (and singing). Remember to pause, in any case, before the first "Christmas is a-comin'" to signal a change of character and voice. Also, you can easily turn the last four measures of each verse into an audience singalong.

The advised tempo is moderately slow until the last line, which is slower. Also, the dynamics are steady, *mezzo forte* (*mf,* which means medium loud) and *mezzo piano* (*mp,* which means medium soft); so, as much fun as you may be having, resist the urge to hop onto a runaway train.

The Christmas Song (Chestnuts Roasting on an Open Fire) (page 28)

Blessed with impeccable timing and a smooth, mellow timbre, Mel Tormé was known during his heyday as "the Velvet Fog." Of more than 300 compositions Tormé wrote throughout his career, nearly half share writing credits with a man named Robert Wells. In 1946, the duo took just half an hour to write "The Christmas Song," one of the most recorded of all Christmas classics. Of course, the man responsible for popularizing the tune was Nat King Cole, who recorded it four separate times between 1946 and 1961, the definitive one being the last, the song's first stereo recording. Of the hundreds who cut renditions, only one other artist besides Cole charted — Christina Aguilera in 1999.

Unless you're a sight-reader extraordinaire (and even then), you need to spend some time practicing all the nuances of this song. Follow the dynamics and tempo markings. Also, remember it's in *cut time* (4/4 that is really 2/2). Nevertheless, the melody is so well-written that you can easily hear how the song should go. The best way to play it is to just express yourself!

Talk about a winter wonderland of chords! Although the key signature denotes E♭, this tune effortlessly uses a wide variety of unique chords. Accidentals, new sharps, and many extra flats enable these forays without changing key signatures. This song is perhaps the most musically rich Christmas standard, and a favorite of many pianists and listeners. Put learning this song on your to-do list immediately. Not the easiest, but well worth the time and effort.

Christmas Time Is Here (page 31)

Vince Guaraldi's sublime piano work is synonymous with Charles Schulz's *Peanuts* animated series. But his story goes much deeper than that. His first recorded work can be heard on *The Cal Tjader Trio,* in 1951 when he was 33. Guaraldi then avoided studios for the next few years, preferring to build his chops on San Francisco's beatnik club scene. In 1955 he put together his own trio. He got his big break in 1963 when he received a gold record and a Best Instrumental Jazz GRAMMY award for "Cast Your Fate to the Wind," a brilliant, accessible piano piece written for *Jazz Impressions of Black Orpheus.* "I don't think I'm a great piano player," Guaraldi once told an interviewer, "but I would like to have people like me, to play pretty tunes and reach the audience. And I hope some of those tunes will become standards. I want to write standards, not just hits." I'd say he definitely got his wish.

Scoot over to the instrumental near the end of the song (where the words stop) and get familiar with it. It's a little trickier than the rest. Then back up and begin your jazz odyssey.

The squiggly line at the beginning is just a rolled chord, also called a *broken chord* or *arpeggio.* Start at the bottom and roll the notes up (play them quickly but separately). Easy, right? Next, you see a crossed-out C note, called a *slashed grace note.* The slash means it's played very quickly (unlike a regular grace note, which is held a little longer). Finally, you stumble upon two *accidentals* . . . not *real* accidents, they're actually meant to be there. For the moment, they override the key signature. The symbol next to the B in the first measure is called a *natural,* just meaning it's not flatted *this* time. The other accidental is the D♭ in the second measure, meaning it *is* flatted *this* time. Now, just play all that jazz.

Impress your friends. Now that you play jazz tell them that the melody for this song is based on extended chords, namely the seventh, ninth, eleventh, and thirteenth as opposed to most pop music which centers its melody around the root, third, and fifth. They may have no idea what you mean, but will likely nod their heads anyway, admiring your great intellect!

Deck the Hall (page 34)

The music to "Deck the Hall" is Welsh in origin and came from a tune called "Nos Galan" dating way back to the 16th century. In the 18th century, Mozart used the tune for a violin and piano duet. During the Victorian reinvention of Christmas, the tune was turned into a traditional English Christmas song. J.P. McCaskey is sometimes credited with the lyrics of "Deck the Hall," but he merely edited the *Franklin Square Song Collection* in which the lyrics were first published. In fact, the author is unknown, but the words are said to originate in America.

Enjoy this nice arrangement of a holiday classic. A good opportunity lies here to work on *voicing* a melody. Let the melody stand out from the accompaniment. Because the right hand plays mostly chords, the top note needs to be voiced slightly louder. Like an orchestra conductor signaling "up" to increase the volume of a principal instrument or singer, the melody needs to be sung out (with your fingers) so it won't be lost among the accompanying chords.

Some arrangements don't include the nice passing chords you see here. Chords such as D minor, G minor, and G7 make this a nice solo piece without too much complexity or too many frills. Also notice the alternate bass notes where the third or fifth replaces the root in the bass. In the introduction the F chord uses the bass note A, which is the third, and later the fifth: C. Use the guitar chords to find these spots by searching for F/A and F/C.

Do You Hear What I Hear (page 36)

Originally recorded in 1962 by the Harry Simeone Chorale, the same bunch that gave us the definitive version of "The Little Drummer Boy," "Do You Hear What I Hear" was written by Noel Regney and his wife Gloria Shayne in 1962. It has been recorded in more than 120 versions, and in almost as many musical styles. In an interview before his death in 2002, Regney said his favorite version was Robert Goulet's. When Goulet came to the line "Pray for peace, people, everywhere," he almost shouted the words. In fact, Regney wrote the song as a clear and plaintive plea for peace at the time of the Cuban missile crisis, in October 1962. Ironically, Regney has an interesting military past. He was drafted into the Nazi Army despite being a Frenchman. He quickly deserted and joined a group of French resistance fighters. While still with the Germans, he once intentionally led his platoon toward a group of French partisans and was shot. All of this background info should make it abundantly plain that this song came from his heart!

This wonderful plea for peace takes a hopeful but reverent tone. Note how the music, not just the lyrics, also tells the story of resolving strife. In the introduction, the darker Gm7 resolves to the bright C major chord while the ominous bass line denotes uncertainty in the world. However, the bass line changes during the hopeful sections. Notice how the bass notes become steady under the lyrics and are even replaced by mid-range chords for the question, "Do you see what I see?"

The key of C is back! It was your best friend in those beginners' books. You soared high without sharps or flats to worry about. Then all those fancy keys came along. Good to see old C again. Nothing is wrong with it.

Review the ending and decide whether or not to play the optional octaves. Remember, if you can't nail it in practice, don't try it in performance. If you *can* manage the big ending, go for it.

Feliz Navidad (page 39)

Year after year, holiday after holiday, you hear José Feliciano's unstoppably joyous tune, one of the season's modern classics and, according to ASCAP, one of the top 25 most played and recorded Christmas songs around the world. It has been covered by everyone from the Cheetah Girls to the Three Tenors, but no one does it like Feliciano. Of the thousands of holiday tunes available at iTunes, "Feliz Navidad" is the #2 most often downloaded holiday song of all time, outselling names synonymous with Christmas like Andy Williams, Elvis Presley, Nat King Cole, and Bing Crosby. Not surprisingly, it's also the biggest selling Latin song on iTunes, period! For Feliciano, that's a lot of *felicidad!*

Need to liven up Christmas at Grandma's? Get that left hand moving with this infectious bass-line beat, and folks will start to sway or even cut a rug (that's an old expression for dancing, kids). Helpful hint: Practice the left and right hands separately if you find this tune tricky. Then *slowly* play both hands together. My piano teacher drove me crazy, making me play pieces slow-ly and cor-rect-ly . . . (yawn). But guess what? It really works. Now bring it up to speed and let the fun begin!

The singing range of this piece makes it a nice solo vocal in the tenor range. The F♯ in the chorus is a great full-voice high note for José Feliciano or your favorite tenor. Sure, opera singers can hit high A and high C with a full voice, that's why they're opera singers. But most pop singers switch to falsetto in that range. So, when playing this arrangement, resist the temptation to announce, "Everybody, sing along!" Don't worry, they'll shout the two lines they know anyway and be happy to groove to the rhythm. That's the party spirit!

The First Noel (page 42)

The origin of this tune is unknown. It's generally thought to be from 16th century England, but possibly goes as far back as the 13th century. Because of the word "Noel," many believed it came from France. But the original spelling of the song, way back in the song's infancy, was "Nowell," the Anglo-Saxon spelling of the word, which makes it, if anything, really "olde!" "The First Noel" was first published in 1833 when it appeared in a collection of seasonal carols, *Christmas Carols Ancient and Modern,* by William B. Sandys. The folio featured extra lyrics, ten verses in all, tacked on by a guy named Davies Gilbert. Many of the extra lyrics aren't included in modern performances,

Stately, steady, and kingly chords ring out for the first noel, which, by all reports, was the best noel of all. The right hand carries both melody and rhythm here. Take a little time to figure out the fingering. The top fingers of your right hand need to stretch a little to make the melody . . . umm . . . melodic. Pencil in 3, 4, or 5 above the chord to remember which finger should take the top note (with the thumb and second finger often playing the bottom two notes).

Note the markings called *slurs* (connected notes) in the vocal above the piano score. This is common when *one* word has *two* or more notes. Words like "the" and "first" each have two melody notes and "Noel" has three notes. Try to make these notes run together as smoothly as possible. Legato fingering with use of the sustain pedal can help you make these chords pronounced without being choppy. Now proclaim!

Frosty the Snow Man (page 44)

After Gene Autry, better known to many as "the Singing Cowboy," sold two million copies of his folksy version of "Rudolph the Red-Nosed Reindeer" in 1949, he was in search of a follow-up holiday hit. Songwriters Jack Rollins and Steve Nelson responded with this equally magical tune for kids, which became a smash for Autry the very next holiday season. "Frosty" possessed all of the secular elements of "Rudolph" and has since followed in its snowy footprints through history, with a short film, an animated special, and a loyal following among children of all ages. I'm still trying to figure out how Frosty's "button nose" turned into a carrot, though. Thoughts?

Don't forget to have fun! With all the work involved in playing the piano, many pianists get too serious. Don't let that happen with this zippy piece! Leave a few bottom notes out if you're still learning or sight-reading, but keep the melody going. Look around and smile at the audience. That's a big part of performing, too.

The left hand uses a *walking bass.* The low notes of the left hand walk up and down the notes of the scale. Many jazz pianists use this technique because, as here, it keeps the song moving in between the melody. Run through it to get the feel. Sometimes, between bass notes, you play almost every note in between (called *moving chromatically).* This sounds cool but may trick your fingers at first.

You songwriter types may want to pay attention to the odd structure of this one. The chorus (the memorable, repeating part: "Frosty the snow man . . . ") tells the story. So no verses are needed. But a bridge (the back story) fills us in: "There must have been some magic . . . " The ending is completely different ("thumpety-thump-thump") and resembles a stage-exiting theater vamping technique with big V-I cadences. Hey, what would you like him to do? He's melting!

God Rest Ye Merry, Gentlemen *(page 50)*

Because the Protestant churches of England and America were closely aligned during the Victorian era, caroling became as popular in America as it was in England. Queen Victoria apparently adored carols! It was during this time that the traditional English carol, "God Rest Ye Merry, Gentlemen," became known in its modern form in America. The song remains popular to this day. Not quite danceable, the tune's durable melody strikes the proverbial Christmas chord, and its lyrics beautifully express the essence of the holiday. Although the author is unknown, many people relate the carol to author Charles Dickens who used it in his book *A Christmas Carol* in 1843. ". . . at the first sound of 'God bless you merry, gentlemen! May nothing you dismay!' Scrooge seized the ruler with such energy of action, that the singer fled in terror, leaving the keyhole to the fog and even more congenial frost." Guess old Ebenezer wasn't all that interested in "resting merrily."

This simple and beautiful piece finds its way onto many recordings in a variety of styles. From up-tempo merry versions to resting mellow renditions, the rich chord changes and enduring message make this a joy to interpret. Although recommended to be played moderately, add your own flavor, whether it's more expressive or more restrained. Find out if you are more Beethoven or Bach!

Play the chorus ("O tidings . . . ") a few times first. By doing so, you get a different sense of the flow of the song. The verses build to the chorus, so you need to hold back a little at first so that the chorus can shine in all its glory.

Notice the juxtaposition of major and minor chords reflecting struggle and hope. What irony that the word "joy" falls on a D minor chord. Many jazz and blues artists cover this olde English carol, changing chords (swapping major and minor or adding sevenths and ninths) and improvising new themes.

Grandma Got Run Over by a Reindeer *(page 52)*

As the story goes, in December of 1978, songwriter Randy Brooks caught Elmo and Patsy Shropshire's act at a Hyatt in Lake Tahoe. After the show, he informally auditioned the Christmas track and the artists had him make a cassette of the recording for them. The duo had the record out by the next year and it became an immediate seasonal hit. If you find a song about an elderly woman who got drunk and, well, killed, on her way home to take her medication a bit peculiar for the holidays, just be glad no one is asking you to play this record's 1982 B-side, "Percy, the Puny Poinsettia." "Grandma" has sold enough copies that old Elmo, since divorced from his singing partner Patsy, has milked this cash cow repeatedly, rerecording the song solo first in 1992 and again in 2000. This addition to the western musical canon appeals to kids and many adults. Print out the lyrics and wrangle some baseball-cap-wearing guys for the best (and worst) singalong you ever did hear!

What? There's technical stuff? Maybe the beginning reference to "Jingle Bells" in a minor key portends looming misfortune? But before you get too cocky about performing this one, check out the key change at the end. It's called a *modulation* and it moves the key up a full step from E to F♯. That is sure a lot of sharps, *dang* near six in all. Practice this part or you'll lose your way before the big ending!

Happy Christmas, Little Friend *(page 56)*

Written by Richard Rodgers and Oscar Hammerstein in 1953, "Happy Christmas, Little Friend" was most famously recorded by Rosemary Clooney backed by Paul Weston and His Orchestra. It was selected as the official 1953 Christmas Seal Song. It also happens to be the only Christmas song Rodgers and Hammerstein ever wrote, which gives them a pretty good batting average at turning Christmas songs into hits. Of course, having written *Oklahoma!, Carousel,* and so many of the most successful and beloved musicals of all time, well, they didn't have to worry too much about hitting another home run.

For all you Broadway fans, here's something familiar and appealing. In the key of G, this arrangement can freshen your repertoire after jamming on standards such as "Silent Night" and "Deck the Hall." Try playing this at a party. It's got great emotional value, and who knows? There may be a crooner among your guests just waiting to belt one out!

Don't get too comfortable with the groove. This song changes drastically from 4/4 to 3/4. But don't worry too much either. After that change it remains in triple time until the end.

The structure of this song includes an introductory piece. Then the song itself starts. Italian opera and American theater have a long history of these (often half-sung or spoken) introductory verses. Pop music recordings usually omit these intros, largely because pop music is about getting in, saying something, and getting out. So, few people are familiar with such introductions until they open up that old piano bench and find the stack of sheet music that's been hiding in there for decades.

Happy Holiday *(page 47)*

Director Mark Sandrich, the man who made five of the best Fred Astaire and Ginger Rogers musicals, also made the seasonal classic *Holiday Inn,* the story of a singer-composer (Crosby) who escapes the rat race of big city show business to run a rural inn open only on holidays. The concept is relatively simple, but it provides enough of a backbone to feature 12 new Irving Berlin tunes, including "White Christmas," "(Come To) Holiday Inn," "Let's Start the New Year Right," and this one, "Happy Holiday." The 1942 flick, with a stellar cast and brilliant soundtrack, has become something of a family event à la *It's a Wonderful Life,* only without all the financial angst.

Tick tock tick tock! Hear that clock ticking? How about bells? A twinkling music box, perhaps? The winter wind blowing snow? Pick your visual image from the many brilliant musical motifs. The steady bass notes, the high chords (an octave up) and a breezy melody combine to create crisp images. Talk about painting a musical picture.

Check out the structure of this song. It's two almost identical choruses (without verses) sung in different keys. Like a lullaby, the song includes a lot of calming repetition, and a major 4th drop in key (from E♭ to B♭).

Keep it easy and slow, subtle and restrained. This song's beauty is in its understatement. The listener floats through the snow globe. It's like a wonderful, natural (and legal) holiday "chill pill."

Happy Xmas (War Is Over) (page 60)

Just as "Do You Hear What I Hear" was originally written as a call for peace, so too is this 1971 tune by John Lennon and his wife Yoko Ono. Both songs have since become Christmas standards. The song was recorded in New York City, with the delightful assistance of the Harlem Community Choir. The single was released in America in December of that year, but delayed a year in the UK due to a publishing dispute. After John Lennon's murder in December of 1980, the song was rereleased right before the holiday and it went to #1. Here's an odd bit of trivia: This song is rarely credited as a #1 song because, even though it topped the charts, the singles chart was never published the week after Christmas. Thus, it has become known as Lennon's secret #1.

Practice the ending to perfect a graceful finish. Most recorded songs fade out, but playing live is different. Slow a little to let the ending notes (some new ones) ring out. Instill the warm feeling the song intends.

Although not a Beatles song, it has a Beatles vocal range (no problem for solo piano). But, if you're planning to sing it, the notes go nearly two octaves above middle C, perfect for a first tenor (like John Lennon). So, try singing it before you hop on the stage at "talent night."

Welcome to world of 12/8. The Ramones could only count to four. (They joked it was their only skill.) Could one of the Beatles really count to 12? Almost. Here's the trick: count to three *four* times. So it's 1–2–3, 1–2–3, 1–2–3, 1–2–3. No pauses, just put a little emphasis on the *one*. Why didn't they just count to 12? Easy — because 11 has three syllables!

Hard Candy Christmas (page 64)

Carol Hall wrote this number for the soundtrack of the 1978 smash Broadway musical *The Best Little Whorehouse in Texas.* Hall, herself a recording artist in the early '70s, wrote all the music and lyrics for this musical as well as the *Whorehouse* sequel and a handful of other well-known '70s tunes, including "A Very Simple Dance," which appeared on the *Sesame Street* children's program. Hall also adapted the music of the play to the film of *The Best Little Whorehouse in Texas,* which starred Dolly Parton as "Miss Mona," the Madam. This particular tune, "Hard Candy Christmas," was released as a Parton single in 1982 and it hit the Top Ten on the country singles charts.

This uber-ballad pulls out all the stops. It's jazzy and tender, full of heartfelt soul-searching. With this type of song, remember not to overdo the sentimentality. If you just play the song the music will do the work.

If you're playing one of those newfangled digital pianos, this would be the perfect time to use a preset sound that combines piano with strings . . . very schmaltzy. Those background violins and cellos fit very nicely here what with all the hard luck sentiment.

Hark! The Herald Angels Sing (page 68)

This one goes way back to 1739, and was written by Charles Wesley, brother of religious icon John Wesley. But Wesley originally wrote it as a sacred poem, not a song. The musical version you know and love today comes courtesy of Felix Mendelssohn in 1840.

Go easy when playing this one! The song is talking about angels singing, not Vikings. Chords like these are often hammered out by pianists, but that is not needed here. You don't want the single melody notes to be overshadowed.

Notice that the melody actually resides in the top note of the chords! Voice those melody notes a little louder than the rest of the chord. Your piano teacher will be proud. You did learn something!

You can find a lot of harmonic stuff to like here. The chord elements, although all present, are spread out to create the fine empty spaces of a Zen garden. The missing notes of the right hand triad are often found in the left hand. Look at the first few measures. The missing C of the first triad is in the bass. Likewise, the B in the E7 chord is down below too. Finally, look at the first G/B chord (measure 3). Here too, the notes of the chord are spread out (in intervals of a fourth and fifth) with B in the bass clef. This trend continues throughout the song. This arrangement features an economy and sparseness that make it absolutely angelic.

Here Comes Santa Claus (Right Down Santa Claus Lane) *(page 70)*

Yes, to most people Gene Autry is both "the Singing Cowboy," and "Mr. Christmas" as well. His holiday hits have featured characters such as "Rudolph," "Frosty," and "Santa Claus." This one, "Here Comes Santa Claus," was Autry's first holiday recording and an immediate hit when it was released in 1947. The story of this song's inspiration is an interesting one. Beginning in 1928, the Hollywood Chamber of Commerce rang in the Christmas season with a parade, called "The Santa Claus Lane Parade." Its first float was, logically, Santa Claus. A spectator, or perhaps a guest, at the parade, Autry heard kids shouting, "Here comes Santa Claus! Here comes Santa Claus," as they watched the bearded celeb approach on his float. The chant inspired him to write this tune with co-author Oakley Haldeman.

Scan the piece to get to know your *accidentals* — extra sharps, flats, and naturals that aren't covered by the E♭ key signature. Think of them as little detours from the key. Practice those parts so that you're not fishing for notes when they arrive. Try not to stop. Nobody likes a stopper who pauses to find the right notes. Better to fumble through with a couple mistakes. It's icy on Santa Claus Lane.

Don't be afraid to bust right into this piece. It's not a subtle song. For fun, finesse the intro a little and then bang away. But the chorus ("Here comes Santa Claus . . . ") comes *before* the verse ("Bells are ringing . . . "), so make the verse a little softer than the big, boisterous chorus.

Although this arrangement looks straightforward, it includes a lot of *passing chords* (in-between chords that get you from point A to point B). This tune uses a neat progression: IV–V–VI–II–V–I. You can see it in the introduction and in the verse. This intricate progression represents Santa's detailed preparations! The big bouncy chorus is good old Saint Nick waddling down the lane. See, you can find rhyme and reason to these madcap songs after all!

A Holly Jolly Christmas *(page 72)*

When the subject of Burl Ives comes up, many of us think of him as the narrator on the much-loved children's special *Rudolph the Red-Nosed Reindeer*. He was the spiffy guy called Sam the Snowman, remember? Anyway, Ives actually did experience quite a successful career prior to that show, acting on both the stage and the screen. He won an Academy Award for *Big Country* as Best Supporting Actor back in 1958 and a GRAMMY Award for Best Country Song in 1962 for "It's Just My Funny Way of Laughin'." He was also an important folksinger during the '50s, with a couple of hit songs. His career spanned more than half a century. But today, Ives' immortality lies in his holiday appearances, which just happen to come around every year. (How often do you hear "It's My Funny Way of Laughin'" compared to, say, songs from *Rudolph the Red-Nosed Reindeer?* Today, "Holly Jolly Christmas," written by Johnny

Marks, also the composer of "Rudolph" and six other tracks expressly written for the Rankin/Bass animated special, is one of his best-loved songs. Ives has come to be known as much for his rendition of this song as Bing has come to be associated with "White Christmas."

 Hop right into this one. It's straightforward and bouncy. Fast quarter notes call for a *cut time* signature (note the c with a slash through it), also called 2/2. The only break comes at the bridge ("Oh ho, the mistletoe"). Otherwise, plow through this one like Santa downing free cookies and milk.

Lots of high-energy Christmas songs use the chorus as a verse. This one is structured chorus–chorus–bridge–altered chorus. Then the whole thing repeats. It's just that easy.

"Holly Jolly Christmas" is a dynamite singalong, but *only* if you bring printed lyric sheets. The range is perfect and everyone loves to shout along. I've played this song for groups many times and, take it from me, it's a sure bet. Make certain to have your tip jar in plain view on the piano!

(There's No Place Like) Home for the Holidays *(page 75)*

This Robert Allen and Al Stillman tune, sung comfortably by the cardigan-wearing Perry Como, came out in 1954 and hit the Top Ten that year. Como hit the charts again in 1957 with his swingin' rendition of "Jingle Bells." As a composer and arranger, Allen frequently accompanied Como. Stillman served as Allen's lyricist, and this tune is one of the trio's best-loved collaborations. In fact, the song was so well received, they decided to recut it in 1959. On the original 1954 version and the remake, the Ray Charles Singers — Ray Charles is rumored to have been in attendance at the session as well — accompanied Como in the studio.

 Get yourself some southern comfort (the feeling, I mean). This song requires a slow, southern lilt to make it work. Often sung by a choir, it has a peaceful community feeling, which is also reflected in the lyrics. So, hang behind the beat a little to create rhythmic anticipation.

This music depicts an era. The prevalence of major chords reflects the optimism and innocence of a time when automobile travel was a joy, as was seeing fellow Americans filling up the open, near-empty roads.

 Practice the verse first. It begins, "I met a man . . . " Wait a minute! Where's the verse? Surprise! The verse is in the middle. As in many holiday classics, the chorus precedes (sometimes even replaces) the verse. Because the chorus is so familiar, it's usually easier to figure out how to play it.

I Heard the Bells on Christmas Day *(page 80)*

"I Heard the Bells on Christmas Day" is a Christmas carol based on the poem "Christmas Bells," composed by Henry Wadsworth Longfellow in 1864. Longfellow, who gets a co-writing credit on this elegant tune, wrote "Christmas Bells" on Christmas Day 1864 in the midst of America's Civil War. Longfellow had just heard the news that his son had suffered wounds as a soldier in battle and he wrote this in what could only be called a blue mood. Interestingly, Longfellow's "Bells" has been set to several tunes. The first was in the 1870s by an English organist, John Baptiste Calkin, to his composition "Waltham." Johnny Marks, known of course for his "Rudolph" composition, set Longfellow's poem to music in this version from the 1950s. Marks' version has been recorded numerous times by various artists, including Kate Smith, Frank Sinatra, Harry Belafonte, and Johnny Cash, and is generally considered to be the song's de facto version.

If the beginning doesn't sound right, take a moment to look at the clefs. They're dual treble clefs. Now combine that with the octave jump in the right hand and check the notes. *Voila!* You've got it!

This pretty tune doesn't like its key. Sure, the key signature indicates F. But by measure five you've got Bm7♭5 and E7 chords. These hardly belong in the average F major key. But F-friendly chords nearby link the odd ones. Connecting the unusual chords with chords that are more at home in a given key is one way composers change tonal centers without changing keys. The result can be interesting and surprisingly nice, as in this Christmas classic.

Because a *legato*, or smooth, fingering is difficult for many progressions, this song is a great opportunity for you to practice pedaling. The key to pedaling is your ear — avoid abrupt stops or blurred measures. But no set rules exist. Rubinstein, the great pianist, once said, "Play it with your nose if you'd like. Just make it sound good!"

I Saw Mommy Kissing Santa Claus *(page 82)*

One thing about classic songs, especially holiday classics, is that they sell again and again and again. "I Saw Mommy Kissing Santa Claus," written by Tommie Connor, has reportedly sold over 60 million records since its initial release. Jimmy Boyd, the young performer whose voice made Connor's song a hit, started his life as a Mississippi farm boy. He was discovered at age 7 at a barn dance, and soon became the talk of the state. He and his family journeyed to Los Angeles when his dad needed a cataract operation. While there, Jimmy entered a talent show (as a singer and guitar player) and won! He became a regular performer on a local talk show and by the age of 12 he was appearing on Frank Sinatra's variety show. Just shy of 13, Jimmy released this song, and it sold an unprecedented 2.5 million copies in its first week! For an encore, Hollywood movies and television appearances followed, and Jimmy was a seasoned star by age 14.

Make this song playful and be sure to bring out, or *voice*, the melody. Keep it moving because *cut time* (symbolized by the c with the line through it, meaning 2/2) means lots of quick notes. It's a good range for singalongs, but be sure to bring lyric sheets!

Sure, this song looks easy! C major, no problemo, bro! But what's with all these flats and sharps? *Accidentals* (sharps, flats, and naturals) make this tune a trickster so do your prep work finding and trying those altered chords. They're easy to find. Look for little clusters of accidentals.

I'll Be Home for Christmas *(page 85)*

Of course everybody wants to be home for the holidays, right? Especially if you're away at war, which was happening to many soldiers exactly when this song hit the airwaves. On October 4, 1943, Bing Crosby recorded "I'll Be Home for Christmas" with the John Scott Trotter Orchestra for Decca Records. The song hit the music charts and remained there for 11 weeks, peaking at #3. It found a tender place in the hearts of Americans, both soldiers and civilians, all of whom were feeling the stress of World War II. The timing, and the gorgeous tune, earned Crosby his fifth gold record. "I'll Be Home for Christmas" became the most requested song at Christmas USO shows in both Europe and the Pacific, and the GI magazine *Yank* said Crosby accomplished more for military morale than anyone else of that era. In December 1965, having just completed the first U.S. space rendezvous and set a record for the longest flight in the space program, astronauts Frank Borman and James Lovell hurtled back to Earth aboard their Gemini 7 spacecraft. When NASA communication personnel asked what tune they wanted piped up to them, the two requested Bing's "I'll Be Home for Christmas."

Skip the introduction! If you're pressed for time, dive right into the familiar part. I won't tell anyone and most likely no one will notice.

This song is harmonically rich. Check out the sus (suspended) chords along with diminished sevenths, flatted fifths, and ninths. But it always comes *home* to the root. Note how the chords hang and blend into one another especially the II-V (Dm7-G7). Great tune.

"I'll Be Home for Christmas" works as a straight-ahead ballad. But if you have a band, tell them to put a little country-western slant on it. You'll have a blast!

It Came Upon the Midnight Clear *(page 88)*

Edmund H. Sears originally wrote these words as a poem, reportedly at the request of his friend W.P. Lunt, a minister in Quincy, Massachusetts. Sears wrote it as a melancholy reflection on his tenure as a Unitarian minister in Wayland, Massachusetts. (In fact, he wrote a number of theological pieces that influenced liberal Protestants in the 19th century.) The hymn was first recited at an 1849 Sunday School Christmas celebration. In the late 1850s, American musician Richard Storrs Willis, a composer who trained under Mendelssohn, was so inspired by Sears' poetry, he put it to music.

 Here's a neat recipe for a homemade introduction. Notice that the introduction is the same as the last few measures of the song. It's a textbook example of turning the end of a song into the intro. Accompanists do it to cue the singer. So, next time you need a moment before the next song, play the last few measures first.

Notice the *slurs*, the curved lines that join vocal notes when one syllable has two notes. Practice that fingering (pencil in 1, 3, 4, and so on to indicate which fingers take the note) to make your playing *legato*, or smooth.

It's Beginning to Look Like Christmas *(page 91)*

Robert Meredith Willson wrote "It's Beginning to Look Like Christmas" back in 1951. Willson was a woodwinds player in John Philip Sousa's band back in the early '20s and in the New York Philharmonic under Arturo Toscanini later that same decade. As a composer, he also went on to write the libretto, the lyrics, and the music for *The Music Man,* the 1957 Broadway hit. In addition to this delightful Christmas track, Willson wrote a number of popular songs, including "Seventy Six Trombones," "May the Good Lord Bless and Keep You," and "Till There Was You," which became a hit for the Beatles in 1963. Velvet voices such as Bing Crosby, Johnny Mathis, and Perry Como covered Willson's classic Christmas chestnut.

Don't let the four flats intimidate you. On a car, that would be trouble. But in music, four flats just means the shining key of A♭. *Cut time* (symbolized by a c with the line through it) simply means a fast 4/4 made into 2/2. So, eat your hearty breakfast and start banging this one out. It's a zippy Christmas favorite.

 Notice the neat songwriting trick of using C7 and F7 in the key of A♭. Normally, C minor and F minor chords would occur, but minor chords are sometimes thought of as "sad." Accidentals, however, make these chords major, "happy" sounds, creating harmonic variety while keeping the song bright. Who wants an ominous Christmas? Not me!

 The introduction and the end of the first verse (just before the repeat) are a little tricky. Practice these repeatedly so you're not ambushed by those triplets and chromatics.

Jingle-Bell Rock (page 121)

As the history of popular music goes, there was Elvis Presley, Bill Haley, and Chuck Berry back in 1955 and 1956; each influenced by Fats Domino and Little Richard. But in 1957, armed with a song by Joe Beal and Jim Boothe, a lesser light named Bobby Helms took the flair of early rock 'n' roll, also known as rockabilly, combined it with a jubilant Christmas theme, and *voila!* A massive hit was born. Helms has sold over 100 million copies of this recording over the years, counting two remakes, which were served up in 1965 and 1967. In 1968, Bill Haley himself recorded a version of the song, and sassy Brenda Lee charted the tune in 1964 and 1967. So it seems safe to say that this rockin' Christmas classic has never really gone away. Helms had a reasonably successful career in country music and was ultimately honored with an induction into the Rockabilly Hall of Fame.

Don't ask your favorite hardcore rock band to play this one. It's not that kind of rock, but rather infectious pop fun for kids of all ages. People can't wait to bop out to this song, especially if you have any swing dancers in the crowd.

Spend a little time on the intro. It's a classic and well-known riff, so you want to nail it. Also, bring out the bridge ("What a bright time").

 Unusual structure alert! I'd call this one chorus–chorus–bridge–repeat all, with a truncated bridge at the end. Seems like anything goes with these holiday classics. They surely defy the verse-chorus pop structure!

Jingle Bells (page 124)

Ah, if a secular and traditional Christmas song has ever been written, it must be "Jingle Bells," a universal tune composed by a man named James Lord Pierpont. Originally titled "One Horse Open Sleigh," the song's been making the rounds since its copyright in 1857. Its place of origin is a bit unclear, though a plaque commemorating the "birthplace" of "Jingle Bells" sits on the side of a building in Medford Square in Medford, Massachusetts. Interestingly, Pierpont intended the song to be played at the Thanksgiving holiday service at his church — note that it has no Christmas references — but the tune was so appreciated that Pierpont reprised it at the Christmas services and there was no turning back. Here's wagering that back then folks knew a lot more of the words than folks do today. Seriously though, how many times is this guy gonna crash his sleigh? And here's a new slant: Some musicologists insist that the word "jingle" in this tune is a verb as in "jingle that bell!"

"Jingle Bells" is a nice, straightforward ditty in G major. No big surprises. A great song to start with. Just play away!

This song is in *cut time*, which is marked by a "c" with a line through it. This is a fast 4/4, which should be marked 2/2.

 Need a rest? Take a nice pause on the "Oh" right before the "Jingle bells" chorus. People find this endlessly amusing no matter how many times you do it. Try it!

Joy to the World (page 130)

Like so many of our current Christmas standards, "Joy to the World" has had a long and somewhat winding path to its present state. The words, based on scripture, were written by a man named Isaac Watts, an English Nonconformist pastor and composer, who died in 1748. Watts wrote over 600 hymns, including such classics as "When I Survey the Wondrous Cross" (put to various tunes over the centuries) and "Marching to Zion" (an inspiring singalong during civil rights marches in the '60s). Musically, "Joy to the World" was arranged and adapted by Lowell Mason, who seemed to take it piecemeal from Handel's *Messiah*. Its success lies in the fact that it's virtually universal, an anthem embraced by a myriad of religious denominations.

This song is free of technical and acrobatic challenges. If you're a quick learner, you can get this one down pretty easily!

In the key of D, this song is good for caroling. Everyone knows the first verse, but lyric sheets are definitely needed for the other verses. Trust me. And if you ever sing this one in a group or choir, make sure the "heaven and nature sing" part is in sync. It usually goes awry and heaven and earth don't sing together at all. Oh, cruel irony!

This piece is rhythmic. Don't hold notes too long (unless marked) or go too heavy on the sustain pedal. Keep those rhythms pronounced but brisk.

Let It Snow! Let It Snow! Let It Snow! (page 132)

Like "Jingle Bells," this pop standard doesn't mention Christmas once. But it's come to be freely associated with Christmas. Sammy Cahn, the tune's lyricist, penned the tune along with composer Jule Styne way back in 1945. It's unfair to attribute this song to Bing Crosby alone because Crooner Vaughn Monroe was the first to cut the track in 1946 and the song topped the charts. More than 300 versions have been recorded over the years, in styles ranging from Ella Fitzgerald's to that of the Nashville Superpickers. I love this song and I always chuckle when I hear the lyric "goodbye-ing!"

"Let It Snow!" is a very nice tune disguised as a bit of a novelty. I've heard jazz pianists really knock it out. It's got a bubbly vibe to it that lends itself naturally to jazz, but you don't have to be Art Tatum to tackle it. This version includes all the basics plus some catchy frills. Check out the fun stuff, starting with the graceful slashed chords and dynamite passing chords.

Watch the tempo, which is designated "moderately." Fun songs like this tend to encourage you to speed up. Suddenly, *oops,* it's become a manic chase scene from a silent movie! Enjoy this one with a little eggnog. It always helps!

Try to distinguish the bridge ("when we finally kiss good-night"). The music changes here. Perhaps soften a little and build to where the verse returns.

Little Saint Nick (page 134)

Back in 1964, the Beach Boys set out to make their first holiday album, *The Christmas Album*. But rather than go through the motions by dressing up a bunch of covers in their own style, they actually wrote 5 of the album's 12 songs. One of those tunes, "Little Saint Nick," the lead track on the album, has become a perennial classic, returning year after year and receiving the cover treatment by contemporary pop acts. The song itself is the Beach Boys' tribute to the hot rod sled of a "real famous cat all dressed up in red." The tune was released as a single in 1963, and featured sleigh bells and glockenspiel to punch it up with holiday flair. They left those touches off the album, choosing to emphasize the group's harmony vocals instead.

Beach Boys fans may also detect a whiff of the tune "Little Deuce Coupe," another Beach Boys cut, from which "Little Saint Nick" borrows its rhythm and structure.

Your mission, should you decide to accept it, is to channel the Beach Boys on your piano. Don't fret, guitar players are jealous of the range and versatility of the piano. The main thing is to keep that bass beat pumping over sweet chords and send your listeners on a California vacation. Keep it loose. This sound is "chill," as the kids say.

Because the Beach Boys harmonies were so important, don't worry too much about voicing top notes louder. (I know, I know, I've advised the opposite in every other song.) But the blend of voices is the melody. That's why few singers cover Beach Boys songs. You actually need lots of singers to cover the Beach Boys, or, at the very least, one guy who can sing like a choir.

Notice that the Beach Boys are masters of the *upbeat,* which means vocals start at the end of measures and end early into measures. So beginnings and ends of measures are happening. Yes, this sometimes means that not much is happening in the middle of the measures, but hey, man, it's cool, that's just their sound!

Merry Christmas, Darling *(page 127)*

The Carpenters had tremendous success with their holiday fare and this song was where it all started back in 1966. "Merry Christmas, Darling," composed by Richard Carpenter with words by Frank Pooler, was the duet's first attempt at writing holiday music. Pooler was the choir director at California State University and Karen and Richard Carpenter were both members of his choir. Twenty years later, Pooler suggested that Richard write music for the ballad, which he did, and it's been a popular tune each holiday season since. The tune also got the Carpenters thinking "holiday music," and ten years later they debuted with a full album of seasonal music called *Christmas Portrait.* Chock full of holiday standards and Karen's sweet singing, the recording sold a million copies that first year and has gone on to be one of the Carpenters' best-loved works.

Got melody? You bet. This tune focuses on melody held up by strong chord progressions. The arrangement rightfully lets the melody dominate and even the accompaniment stays subtle. Practice the melody alone. Don't be afraid to vary the tempo a little. Find expression and then add the rest. You'll see why singers love this song!

Mark the coda. It's easy to get caught up and forget to play the right notes or forget where the heck you are. This music makes you feel good!

Would you like some jazz with that? If you want some sweet, smooth jazz, then sample this treat. Start with an *arpeggio* (that squiggly line at the beginning), add lots of minor 6ths, 7ths, and 9ths, descending bass lines, and finally, surprise major chords. That's a recipe for jazz!

Mistletoe and Holly *(page 138)*

Although Frank Sinatra is known for his swingin' interpretations of great material, he also had a hand in writing some tunes on his own. This song, one of the only Christmas tunes he tackled, is written with frequent collaborators Doc Sanford and Hank Sanicola. It was written specifically for *A Jolly Christmas from Frank Sinatra,* a classic holiday album with arrangements and conducting by the legendary Nelson Riddle.

If you're sitting on the bench during the holiday season trying to keep people entertained, chances are you'll get a request or two for something by Ol' Blue Eyes himself, Frank Sinatra. If you do, why not play this one? He wrote it! Or at least cowrote it. So you know it's going to swing. Pure fun in B♭, this bounces in *cut time,* a fast version of 4/4. Make sure you read the lyrics poking fun at Christmas presents, tasty pheasants, and relatives you don't know. You know they had a ball making this one!

Check out the bridge ("Then comes the big night") before you get overly confident. Be ready for lots of *accidentals* (added sharps, flats, and naturals), triplets, and a coda. Get this section down and go back to bopping with, "Oh, by gosh, by golly!"

 Frank Sinatra improvised frequently. A pioneer in an age where conductors and arrangers told the singers and players exactly what to sing or play, Frank added his own twists in terms of beats, invented lines, and changed tempos. In so doing, he created a new show every night. It's surprising that a member of the Rat Pack was so free-spirited and adhered more to a rock 'n' roll ethos than many rockers, even though he despised rock 'n' roll himself. Hats off to Frank! You may be inspired to improvise a few lines yourself!

The Most Wonderful Time of the Year (page 140)

It would be fun to hear composer George Wyle discuss his credentials at say, a cocktail party. "Well, I was the musical director of *The Flip Wilson Show.* I also directed and arranged the music for John Denver and the Muppets' *A Christmas Together.* I wrote a few unusual songs like 'I Said My Pajamas (And Put On My Pray'rs)' back in '49, and 'I Didn't Slip, I Wasn't Pushed, I Fell' the next year. But the one thing I'm most proud of is my work with Sherwood Schwartz on 'The Ballad of Gilligan's Island.' Yep, that's one I'm pretty, uh, proud of." Fortunately for Wyle, he also wrote this timeless celebration of the season, "The Most Wonderful Time of the Year," a song Andy Williams made his own starting in 1963.

Don't be scared by the introduction! It gets a little orchestral and dramatic. Take a deep breath and say "Aaaaa!" Feel better? That's the key — A, with three sharps. After you get past the intro, the song zips along pretty easily. Even the two key changes don't complicate the straightforward melody and chord pattern. After all, it's a wonderful time of the year!

 Watch out for paper cuts! You'll be turning lots of pages. And be sure to wear good shoes, because you're jumping keys twice: to C and B♭.

This is a nice long waltz. Warn grandparents, aunts, uncles, kids, and anyone with *ballroom dancing fever* that they should be prepared to be on the dance floor for a while. The feel goes something like this: *one,* two, three, *one,* two, three . . .

My Favorite Things (page 146)

The wintertime imagery of some of the lyrics — "Bright copper kettles and warm woolen mittens . . . Snowflakes that stay on my nose and eyelashes" — has made "My Favorite Things" a popular song during the holiday season, and it often appears on seasonal compilations. But the irony is that in *The Sound of Music,* the Rodgers and Hammerstein tune is sung by Maria during a summer thunderstorm. From the Broadway stage, the song has also become a standard in popular music, in pop, rock, soul, hip-hop, and country styles. John Coltrane, the free-jazz saxophonist, titled his landmark 1961 album after the tune. In his rendition, he took what is essentially a very cheerful song, and explored avant-garde modal playing, using his soprano sax to solo over the vamps of the two "tonic" chords, E minor and E major. The 14-minute work became Coltrane's most requested tune.

 This song may become one of your favorite things, too! Try the *arpeggio,* or broken chord, in the left hand of the fifth measure. It's different, isn't it? Unless you have giant hands, glide as you roll the chord. Now, that's the sound of music!

After the second verse, the one mentioning "cream-colored ponies," note the quick change to E major and A major. It only lasts a few measures but adds variety and spice to this already great chord progression. Jazz bands dig covering this precisely because of those changes. Find your own style, though, and make this classic your own.

Staccato notes, with the little dot over or under the note, are quick, nonsustained, and very easy to play and read after you get the concept. But stay cool, and don't make everything you play sound staccato. If you do, don't worry. It'll pass.

O Christmas Tree (page 150)

They really get into their evergreens over in Germany. The earliest known version of this ode to the tree dates back almost 500 years, which makes sense considering how simplistic the lyrics are. By medieval times, the tradition of bringing in flowers and trees had been established to honor the birth of the Christ. Despite its ancient "roots," the best-known version of the tune is more contemporary, only going back to 1824 when a Leipzig music teacher named Ernst Anschutz adapted his own rendition to the lyrics. The Vince Guaraldi Trio plays the beloved version found on the animated "Charlie Brown Christmas" special.

Practice the right hand alone for a while. Add the left hand accompaniment later. Listen to how great it sounds when the left hand joins in.

Although the time signature is 3/4, the dotted rhythms and expressive nature of the chords prevent this tune from becoming a waltz. The music box feel does make dancers twirl, but jazz players have co-opted it for the changes and rhythms. So, keep it slow and ambiguous and flexible to interpretation. The dancers will retreat to the bar for drinks and, ideally, throw money in your tip jar along the way!

O Come, All Ye Faithful (Adeste Fideles) (page 152)

Here's another one of those songs with a long-winded history. I'll spare you the gory details and just give you the skinny. It was first published in 1751 by John Francis Wade, in his book of hymns, *Cantus Diversi (Different Songs)*. Although Wade wrote the melody, it is unclear whether he wrote the words, or if he adapted an older text. The tune is known as "Adeste Fideles," Latin for "come, you faithful."

Try playing just the top and bottom notes. Hear the essence of it. Now add the rest. Hear how each element either adds texture or second melody, just as each individual voice adds to a choir? This arrangement needs a choir of fingers (and a conductor). Ready, maestro?

Simplicity and voicing rule the day. You likely have enough jazz and pop carols already in your repertoire, so hold back on this one and treat it traditionally. You'll discover that by doing this, the dynamics *within* the chord will really bring this piece to life!

People often don't realize that *part music* — that is, more than one note sung together — is pretty recent. For a long time, ecclesiastical composition, the force behind much Western music, eschewed musical concepts like pleasure, beauty, and fun. In the olde days, unison songs, that is, songs with one melody, dominated churches. So, close your eyes and drink in this (relatively) new sound.

O Holy Night *(page 154)*

Back in 1847, a composer named Adolphe Adam took Placide Cappeau's French poem called "Minuit, chretiens," and composed "Cantique Noel," or "O Holy Night." A Unitarian minister named John Sullivan Dwight translated the words into English in 1855 and published it in his *Journal of Music*. Years later, on December 24, 1906, a Canadian inventor named Reginald Fessenden broadcast the first AM radio program. The program featured Fessenden on violin playing, of all songs, "O Holy Night." This makes the carol the first song ever to be played on the radio. Wonder if it became a hit? Went platinum?

Rub your belly while patting your head. Got it? Once you've mastered that, get to work on this song. The left hand bass is a neat, repeating figure, but needs lots of practice unless you're a *wunderkind*. Figure out the best fingering technique to keep it smooth. Understand that you're not "rockin' around the Christmas tree" with Brenda Lee here, people!

Watch the dynamics of this composition carefully. Don't go nuts, because the song builds, calms, builds, slows, and so on. Just follow the directions written here: *crescendo* (*cresc.,* which means get slowly louder), *decrescendo* (*decresc.,* which means get slowly softer), *ritardando* (*rit.,* which means slow down), *mezzo piano* (*mp,* which means medium soft), *piano* (*p,* which means soft), and so on.

Play to your heart's content. As for singing, remember that this song is sung by famous tenors. So, if you plan to tackle it in public with your own vocal cords, get some professional guidance. Each year Paul Shaffer, bandleader for the *Late Show* with David Letterman, imitates pop icon Cher's rock 'n' roll version of "O Holy Night," to hilarious effect. It's must-see in a train-wreck kind of way. Don't make the same mistake!

O Little Town of Bethlehem *(page 158)*

Phillips Brooks is best known for writing this tune, though, given his rich past, that's a bit surprising. Born in Boston, Brooks is a descendent of the Reverend John Cotton on his dad's side and Mary Ann Phillips on his mom's, both of whom were from important religious families in the Boston area. In 1869 he became the rector of the famous Trinity Church in Boston, outside of which his statue resides. He was consecrated the Bishop of Massachusetts in 1891 and is today remembered in the Episcopal Church with his own feast day. Nevertheless, in most circles he is known as the man who wrote "O Little Town of Bethlehem" after a trip to the holy city in 1865.

This song also takes you to a place called "Chromatica." *Chromatics* are half-step movements that achieve an airy effect. They illustrate the quiet and humble birth. Practice the right hand patterns to get the feeling.

The use of sixth intervals pervades this song. Fifth and sixth *intervals* (where the middle chord note is dropped) invoke open landscapes or quiet empty streets. Because diatonic scales don't include all 12 Western tones, there is need for accidentals. Nifty effects like this are used to score films. Classically-inclined pianists like Randy Newman use a technique like this with frequency and success.

There is a beautiful moment in this mosaic where the lyric turns, "Yet in thy dark streets shineth/the everlasting light." Accent the contrary motion of bass and treble then return to the parallel motion that distinguishes this classic!

Rockin' Around the Christmas Tree (page 160)

Here's a trivia question: Which happened first: Did Brenda Lee become a star and record this song or did Brenda Lee record this song and then become a star? Johnny Marks wrote this song and recorded it with Brenda Lee back in 1958, *before* Lee was a star. In fact, they released it again in 1959 as well, and it didn't make any impact then either. It wasn't until Brenda Lee hit the Top Ten in 1959/60 with "Sweet Nothin's," "I'm Sorry," and "I Want to Be Wanted" that she was able to make a push with her Christmas hit. In 1960 and 1961 Lee, known as "Little Miss Dynamite," owned pop music with an incredible string of hits. This tune sold well for the next 25 or so years, landing at #5 on the Christmas chart as recently as 1984! Now that's timeless!

Here's your chance to taste a little boogie-woogie piano during the holidays. Most boogie-woogie pianists worth their salt have a left hand that parties all night long. So, if you like the little boogie pattern here with the *slashed grace note* (the crossed out one) call the doctor. You've got boogie-woogie fever and rockin' pneumonia! There's an old saying about blues, stride, and boogie piano which goes, "The left hand is God." If you have that talent, internal clock, and chops, then do it.

Practice the middle section ("You will get a sentimental feeling") separately a few times or you may fall off your piano bench. It's a neat contrast and very pleasant surprise. Can you keep a secret? Sometimes, alone, I play this pretty section all by itself.

Rudolph the Red-Nosed Reindeer (page 166)

Back in 1939, an employee of Montgomery Ward department store named Robert May created a funny-looking reindeer character named Rudolph with a storyline to match. Not long after, May's brother-in-law, Johnny Marks, decided to put Rudolph's story to music. The rest, as they say, is history. Rudolph is now one of popular culture's most familiar characters. Marks, a Jewish artist and veteran of World War II, struck gold with other Christmas tunes, including "Rockin' Around the Christmas Tree" with Brenda Lee, "A Holly Jolly Christmas" with Burl Ives, and "I Heard the Bells on Christmas Day," first and most famously recorded by Bing Crosby.

Notice the double treble clefs to start. The rhythm is briefly "ad lib.," which means "do what you want" until the "A tempo" marking, which means "stop that!" Return to "relatively fast, lightly." Get a move on, Santa!

Notice how economically the arrangement works. Inversions (like jazz pianists use) help change chords. Why bounce to the root chord every time? In the ninth measure, look at the Am to E7/B change. The hands hardly move, yet interesting, close harmonies are created.

"Rudolph" works well as a singalong, but if the singers lose the beat, you may want to *trumpet.* Trumpeting uses *loud* right-hand octaves for the melody to get the singers back on track. Try it. It really does work. Everyone, including reindeer, needs a few magic tricks to take flight!

Santa Baby *(page 170)*

If a pastor, priest, or minister from your church requests a Christmas song, let's just say right now that this would not be the one to play . . . unless it's a very, umm, *hip* church. Orson Welles once called Eartha Kitt the "most exciting woman in the world," which is a high honor indeed. Welles gave Kitt her first starring role, in his 1950 adaptation of *Dr. Faustus*, in which she portrayed Helen of Troy. Kitt used a heap of that excitement while recording the super-sexy vocals for "Santa Baby," the song for which she is best known. And if you're looking for a little Marilyn Monroe trivia you won't find it here. Monroe *never* covered the song. An obscure, breathy-voiced singer named Cynthia Basinet recorded the version often attributed to the Blonde Bombshell.

 This simmering delight attracts blues fans above all. Be careful, they'll tipple and talk and oops, you've lost your place! Stay focused as the chords seem to repeat but actually don't. The A minor chords become A7, which is major, and the melody substitutes notes somewhat randomly. *Play* the blues, baby, don't *get* 'em!

Think you've mastered the first few measures and it's chillin' time? Think again. Flip to the bridge ("Think of all the fun I've missed . . ."). Make sure you can nail the end of the bridge (and not go off it) with its descending chromatics and triplets. Now you're gettin' the blues!

 Don't stop me if you've heard this one before. Does this song sound a little familiar? Hear some "Heart and Soul," "All I Have to Do Is Dream" or "Stormy Weather"? Yup, this chord progression is a staple of pop culture. Variations abound. I-VI-II-V, VI goes minor, II gets replaced by IV and every chord gets "seventh-ed" eventually.

Santa, Bring My Baby Back (To Me) *(page 163)*

Beyond the traditional classic voices of Christmas — Bing, Frank, Dino, and the rest —one other artist ranks up there in terms of his contributions to seasonal music: Elvis Presley. Elvis recorded his best seasonal material at the peak of his early rock 'n' roll artistry in the late '50s, including the two colors of "Christmas" ("White" and "Blue"), one of his patented, hyper-sexual suggestions in "Santa Claus Is Back in Town," and two of his most playful holiday tunes, Gene Autry's "Here Comes Santa Claus" and this one, "Santa, Bring My Baby Back (To Me)." Elvis also did a variety of spiritual carols, making his holiday performances some of the most diverse — with pop, rock, rockabilly, gospel, and blues styles represented — and finest of the popular era.

FAQ: "Can you play something not too depressing?" Yes, you can! Pull out this ditty and have them bopping like cats full of coffee! Bright and moving, this 4/4 stomper lets the first and third beats ring, not relying on off-beats to roll along. No tricky musical devices here, this one's a straight-ahead pop song — finally!

 One little change here is the bridge, but it's pretty normal, with no unexpected passing chords. However, make sure to bring out (voice) the bass notes as their movements add energy. This song's a fun romp.

Santa Claus Is Comin' to Town (page 174)

Fred Coots and Haven Gillespie bumped into each other in 1934 on a Brooklyn subway. Gillespie, a lyricist, had some words he needed to put to music and Coots, a composer, was always looking for lyrical inspiration to help him with his work. The next afternoon, Gillespie handed Coots something he'd been working on. It wasn't much. All he had was a little ditty — a kid song. But Coots took it, hoping that the next one was something more "serious," maybe even a hit. In about ten minutes, Coots pecked out a few notes on the piano. Coots delivered the song to a rather underwhelmed publisher, who reluctantly put it out with virtually no expectations. Later that summer, Coots offered it to Eddie Cantor, a popular singer, who decided to use it on his radio show in November. Suddenly the song shot from nowhere into the hearts and minds of an America that needed a lilt and a lift. The morning after Cantor sang it on the radio, orders came in for 100,000 copies of sheet music. By Christmas, sales had surpassed 400,000.

Imagine that you're the first person ever to play this. You need to *forget* every other version you've heard. Three-chord versions of this common tune abound, but this arrangement includes all the real chords plus a few. Don't let your guitarist tell you, "Dude, my version is better." It may be different, but this one is right on!

Okay, the Bruce Springsteen version is very cool. But that's *his* version. He's "the Boss." If you customize, do *your* own little rap at the beginning. Your fans and friends want you. Be real!

Jump ahead to the bridge ("He sees you when you're sleeping . . . ") and give that a good run-through. Look out for some new chords and *accidentals* (added sharps, flats, and naturals) here. And remember, Santa knows if you've been a bad pianist, so make sure you practice.

Shake Me I Rattle (Squeeze Me I Cry) (page 177)

Marion Worth, born in Birmingham, Alabama, was a popular performer on the Grand Ole Opry in Nashville in the early 1960s. For a few years her hits were traditional country. But in 1963 she crossed over to the pop charts with this endearing holiday tale about a poor little girl with her eye on a doll she sees in a toy shop window. The song doesn't mention Christmas, or even the holiday, but it does speak of it being around winter, which made it a universal seasonal hit on both the pop and country charts. The song was written by Hal Hackaday, a Broadway lyricist with numerous theatrical credits, including *Snoopy!!!*, *Minnie's Boys*, and *Whatever Happened to Baby Jane?*

You know that new digital piano with 500 instrument sounds? Well, now's the time to try the "music box" sound. (Of course, a regular piano will work, too!) A sweet and sentimental waltz in B♭, the lilting, fairly slow melody needs to stay hopeful, letting harmonies introduce longing. Nice melodic jumps help tell this "coming of age" story.

An important marking early on is *ritardando (rit.)*, which indicates a slowing tempo. Also important are the double lines (railroad tracks-like tram lines), which are called *caesuras*, and prescribe a pause.

Don't overdo it! Note that the dynamic is *mezzo forte* (*mf*, which means medium loud). This effect can invoke the sound of a child asking for a toy, but a soft touch goes a long way toward making this child sweet and deserving. Asking with too much gumption easily crosses into "spoiled brat" territory, which is not the desired result. So, make it sweet and unassuming and keep your heart open wide!

Silent Night *(page 180)*

A beloved carol, "Silent Night" also has a beautiful story to go along with it. The German words for the original six stanzas were written in 1816 by Joseph Mohr, a young priest assigned to a pilgrimage church in Mariapfarr, Austria. On December 24, 1818, Mohr visited musician/schoolteacher Franz Gruber, who lived in nearby Arnsdorf. Mohr showed Gruber the poem and asked him to add a melody and guitar accompaniment so that it could be performed that night at Midnight Mass. They worked on it all day and that evening, the two men, backed by a choir at St. Nicholas Church, sang "Stille Nacht! Heilige Nacht!" for the first time. Part of the miracle of "Silent Night" is its unspectacular origins, and the lovely simplicity of its melody. I doubt that Mohr and Gruber could have imagined the impact their composition would have on the world. It has been translated, at last count, into 130 different languages and contains the season's most powerful message of heavenly peace, one that crosses all borders and barriers.

Roll that bass! Note the contrast of the rolling bass and hypnotic quarter notes. The gathering round is marked by rhythmic eighths while the quarter notes suggest peaceful prayer. Fuller chords brighten certain moments, whereas single notes shade somber sentiments. Little syncopations also help make this a subtle, nuanced "Silent Night."

 Absolutely practice left and right hands separately. Note your fingering patterns for rolling that bass. Also, practice chord jumps in the right hand. With those two skills down, you'll see why this song endures as perhaps *the* Christmas song.

 "Silent Night" is a beautiful song about birth and miracles. A manger, hardly pristine or wondrous, is made perfect by faith. And this song, even now as friends and family join together on Christmas Eve, never fails to bring a tear. So sing this, just one verse, softly at the end of the night. And wish all well.

Silver Bells *(page 182)*

Written as a response to all of the rural-based Christmas songs and the romanticized, bucolic imagery of most holiday music, "Silver Bells" is one of the only tunes to describe what Christmas is like in the Big City, with its department store lights, window displays, and "busy sidewalks." Collaborators Ray Evans and Jay Livingston wrote the song on assignment by Paramount Studios, which was making a movie called *The Lemon Drop Kid.* The film starred Bob Hope and Marilyn Maxwell and needed a Christmas song. The result was a holiday classic, especially after Bing Crosby and Carol Richards recorded it in 1951. Livingston and Evans enjoyed a fruitful creative partnership beyond this composition as well, collaborating on mega-hits such as "Que Será, Será" and "Mona Lisa."

This song assumes you *like* bells, which in some cities can be especially loud and not necessarily on key. Fortunately, you don't have to ring any real bells in this song. But beautiful "piano bells" color the introduction to the prelude. The prelude, however, has enough tempo and dynamic markings to put bats in your belfry. Yes, it's very educational, but the question is, "To prelude or not to prelude?" Read on for pros and cons.

 You can simply skip the prelude. The prelude doesn't repeat, very few people recognize it (the "silver bells" part comes later), and it has a lot of dynamic and tempo markings. But consider keeping the pretty "bell" intro and then moving on to play the more-familiar part.

 Or, when you really want to ring someone's bells, absolutely keep the awesome prelude. Just jot this down! Double treble clefs to start, accented notes (arrows), dynamics: *forte (f,* which means loud), *mezzo forte (mf,* which means medium loud) to *mezzo piano (mp,* which means medium soft), a *rallentando (rall.,* which means slowing gradually), some *caesuras (//,* sometimes called *railroad tracks,* indicating pauses). Finally, where the lyrics start, the song goes back to the initial tempo (*a tempo*), which means "moderately." Not so bad, and it's in B♭, a nice key. At least try it. You might like it!

This Christmas *(page 186)*

More than 100 versions of Donny Hathaway's contemporary classic Christmas tune have appeared since its inception in the early '70s, including covers by Peabo Bryson, Patti LaBelle, the Whispers, the Dramatics, Diana Ross, Christina Aguilera, and Destiny's Child. Many even refer to it as the last great Christmas song, and put it on the short list of contemporary Christmas classics, alongside very few others. Hathaway himself, a soul prodigy and one of the era's true musical geniuses, was also something of an enigma. He made some of the most memorable soul of the soul-heavy '70s, and deserves to be considered alongside contemporaries such as Aretha Franklin, Curtis Mayfield, and Marvin Gaye. But he never achieved the commercial success of those artists, and, frustrated, left this world at the age of 34, a suicide victim.

While this wonderful piece a bit more difficult than some of the other tunes in this book, don't panic! Notice that the introduction uses the same two-bar pattern three times — learn it once, play it thrice! Learn the tricky rhythms by practicing the hands separately. After you get past the intro, you will be happy to see that the verses and choruses are simpler. More good news: After the verse and chorus, that two-bar pattern from the introduction returns.

The Twelve Days of Christmas *(page 190)*

For those who enjoy a little trivia, the festival relating to the "Twelve Days of Christmas" is pretty ancient. It's based on the tradition that it may have taken 12 days for the three kings, also called the wise men, to get to Bethlehem after Jesus was born. So these 12 days start on Christmas Day itself and run until January 5, literally the Twelfth Night, and the eve of Epiphany. Some suggest that the lyrics are a form of Christian instruction dating to the 16th-century religious wars in England, when some Catholics had to veil references to the basic teachings of their faith. "A partridge in a pear tree," for example, is Jesus; "two turtledoves" refers to the Old and New Testaments of the Bible; "four calling birds" hints at the four gospels, and so on.

The music for this super-familiar song is borrowed from a children's rhyme originating from 18th-century London. It evolved from a memory game in which a group of kids would take turns saying the first line and additional lines without flubbing them. Years later, the rhyming game was adopted into a fun family singalong every Twelfth Night in England.

If you don't like this song, allow me to change your mind right now! As a pianist, this tune is, and will forever be, your friend. It can also make you one popular player because it's a fantastic singalong. Trust me, just print up lyric sheets, practice, and put it smack in the middle of your Christmas party song set. People love singing it because it's long and repeats and someone always comes up with a really funny stab at "Five golden rings!" You may even want to memorize it — that way you can have a blast right along with your chorus!

Welcome to the land of codas. This isn't brain surgery, but you definitely need to figure out the sequence. Also, note how the rhythm alternates between 4/4 and 3/4. Fortunately, you know this song, so you can hear how it needs to go! Now just play it!

Discover the piano *trumpeting technique.* Notice the single melody notes in the vocal staff. Put your thumb on that note and your fifth finger an octave up. Now play that melody with *all* octaves. When needed (for loud off-key singing), get the singers back on track with loud melody octaves. Then return to your normal accompaniment.

We Wish You a Merry Christmas *(page 193)*

In the days of Merrie Olde England, much of life was accompanied by the sounds of music. Wealthy merchants hired bands to join them on walks through town. Hawkers enhanced their sales pitches by belting out attention-getting songs, and municipal choruses were licensed to enliven weddings of the rich, or sing in the square day and night. These choruses were especially busy around Christmas, when they'd serenade citizens on snowy nights, turn the Nativity story into song, and make spirits brighter and the holiday merrier. In return, they might receive coins, or a bit of spiced ale or roasted pig. Many of the oldest carols come from this singing tradition, including this one, which hails from the West Country of England, around the 16th century. Though I'm still not sure about what "figgie pudding" actually tastes like.

Keep the song going with rhythmic consistency: chorus-verse-chorus-verse-chorus, and so on. It has a perfect singalong range, so be sure to add it to your set. The version included here even has extra lyrics for the super-ambitious. But a word of warning: This song can be addictive to your musical health and you may get more "figgie pudding" from appreciative listeners than you can eat.

 You may hear musicians mention a *circle of fifths,* which means that the next chord is a fifth up from the present one. In Western music, the fifth element of a scale is called the *dominant.* A chord built on the dominant is the strongest chord change. The fourth is next, called the *sub-dominant.* When you recognize that this tune is built (mostly) around a circle of fifths, you can see it's a great way to master common chord progressions.

What Are You Doing New Year's Eve? *(page 196)*

The title of this song is the musical question introducing Frank Loesser's fine 1947 pop standard, one of the Christmas season's most touching ballads and a song (and query) still heard today. Top recording artists still take a crack at this one, most prominently roots country singer Lee Ann Womack and jazz pianist Diana Krall. Throughout his illustrious career, Loesser wrote the lyrics to over 700 songs. He wrote and composed the Pulitzer-prize winning musical *How to Succeed in Business Without Really Trying* and the masterful *Guys and Dolls,* which won a Tony Award for Best Musical in 1951. Loesser also earned an Academy Award for Best Song in 1949 for another memorable winter holiday standard, "Baby, It's Cold Outside."

The hopeful and amiable lovebird in this holiday classic is well loved, even though the character stutters a bit (notice the dotted-eighth notes), talks too fast (see the triplets), and begins most measures with an "awkward pause" (that is, a quarter-note rest). But, alas, the hero ultimately musters the courage to pop the *big* question: "What are you doing New Year's Eve?" Make sure to let those big half notes and whole notes ring out. He or she really, really, really wants a date.

 Aside from the neat rhythmic figure, this song also has alternating major and minor chords throughout, heightening the "Yes" or "No" of the courtship pendulum swing. But when the bridge enters ("maybe I'm crazy . . ."), be sure to mark a clear change of tone. The harmonic movement to the *third* of the key signifies staunch determination! Longer notes prevail, too. It's a New Year's Eve date, after all, not lunch at the greasy spoon! Play it like you mean it.

 Don't overdo the angst! Keep it playful and jumpy, obeying the cut time. This fun ditty is a courtship dance, so keep it bright. Those minor chords always do resolve because, come on, with a sweet little proposition like this, who could possibly say "No"?

Wonderful Christmastime (page 199)

Paul McCartney's holiday single from 1979 is one of those songs that divides a musical nation. Like a few other "Macca" tunes — "Ebony & Ivory" and "Ob-La-Di, Ob-La-Da" — "Wonderful Christmastime" is one of those songs that you can either love or loathe, depending on how much cheer you prefer in your music. If you enjoy the chorus here, you're in luck, because the line repeats over 30 times! Back in 1979, a month after the release of "Wonderful Christmastime," McCartney had a bit of a misadventure. He inadvertently made the headlines when he was arrested at Tokyo's Narita Airport for possession of half a pound of marijuana. Not dear Paul!? The former mop-top spent ten days in a Japanese jail before being released and deported. Talk about a holiday buzz kill!

Here's the sneaky part of this song: A single melody (the opening one) repeats four times over four *different* chords. Practice each chord first and the rest of this romp just scoots along.

Sir Paul trots out a common Western chord technique called the *circle of fifths*. "The choir of children" lyric rests atop a Gm-Cm7-F7-B♭ progression. Each change moves down a fifth. This song sails "steady as she goes" in the key of B♭. Mark the *codas* (repeats) and figure out an ending (repeat and fade rarely works live). Maybe a Beatles reference?

Find the song that's right for you! Pop songs by Paul McCartney, David Bowie, Sting, and other stars can be difficult to sing. Some hit songs have repeating melodies that highlight a particular singer's voice, in high ranges, over great instrumental riffs. In those cases, inflection, tone, and power trump melodic composition. McCartney did write great melodies. But this little ditty is no "Long and Winding Road" or "Yesterday." Grab a few friends and belt out "Wonderful Christmastime," but opt for his melodic ballads for your solo recital!

You're All I Want for Christmas (page 204)

Film star, conductor/arranger, jazz pianist, talent scout, DJ, and songwriter are just a few of the roles a man named Seger Ellis played during his productive and successful lifetime. "You're All I Want for Christmas" is one of his standards, along with "No Baby, Nobody but You" and "You Be You but Let Me Be Me." He began playing piano as a kid and began playing professionally, on the radio, in the mid-1920s. He made a few records at this time before encountering, and subsequently managing, the famous vocal group the Mills Brothers. After a stint in the Army, he moved back to his native Texas and became more involved in songwriting, which he also did well. This Christmas chestnut, one of his most successful compositions, received the white-glove vocal treatment from the likes of Al Martino, Frankie Laine, and the ubiquitous caroler, Bing Crosby.

Close your eyes and picture a theater stage. Note the "Ad lib. dreamily" marking. "Ad lib." means "do your thing" but be careful, don't make it too slow. *Cut time* (symbolized by a c with a line through it, or 2/2) indicates movement. Note the early *mezzo piano* (mp, which means medium soft) marking and ending *molto ritardando* (molto rit., which means greatly slowing). But mostly, this one comes from the heart!

Look at the I-IV-V (F-B♭-C) prevalence early on (key of F). But later you see C, F, and Gm. This is no key change, but the dominant V chord (C) has spawned its own I-IV-V. I call this a textbook example of "why the heck is that chord there?"

A short and sweet number, the notes ring out longingly. In the spaces between the melodies, you can find the arranger's moment to shine. Make sure to express those nicely phrased passing chromatic lines to salute the man behind the curtain! Bravo! Bravo!

Jingle-Bell Rock

Words and Music by Joe Beal and Jim Boothe

Copyright © 1957 by Chappell & Co.
Copyright Renewed
International Copyright Secured All Rights Reserved

Jingle Bells

Words and Music by J. Pierpont

Copyright © 1993 by HAL LEONARD CORPORATION
International Copyright Secured   All Rights Reserved

Merry Christmas, Darling

Words and Music by Richard Carpenter and Frank Pooler

Rubato

Greet-ing cards have all been sent, the Christ-mas rush is through,

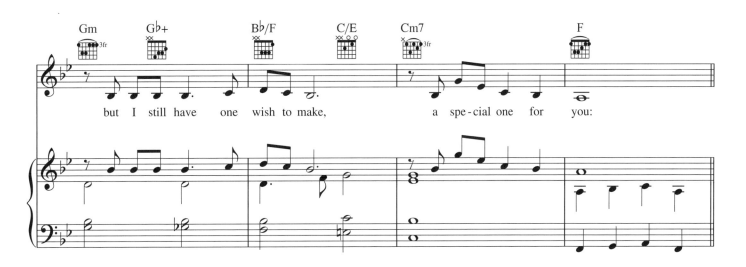

but I still have one wish to make, a spe-cial one for you:

Moderately slow

Mer-ry Christ-mas, dar-ling. We're a-part, that's true; but

Copyright © 1970 IRVING MUSIC, INC.
Copyright Renewed
All Rights Reserved   Used by Permission

Joy to the World

Words by Isaac Watts
Music by George Frideric Handel
Adapted by Lowell Mason

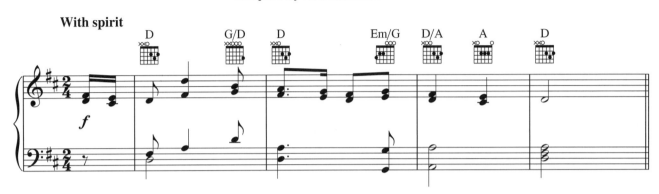

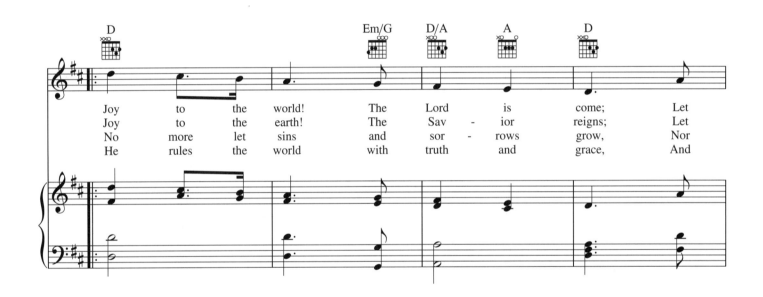

Joy to the world! The Lord is come; Let
Joy to the earth! The Sav - ior reigns; Let
No more let sins and sor - rows grow, Nor
He rules the world with truth and grace, And

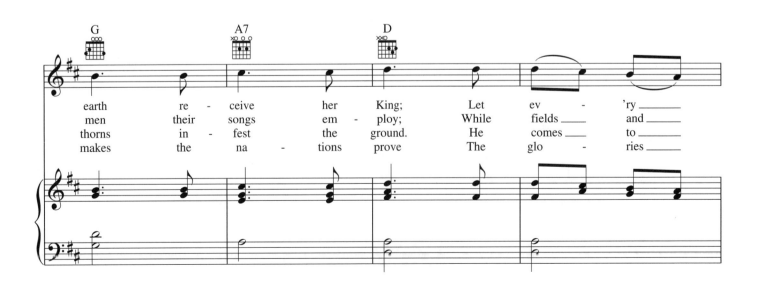

earth re - ceive her King; Let ev - 'ry _____
men their songs em - ploy; While fields _____ and _____
thorns in - fest the ground. He comes _____ to _____
makes the na - tions prove The glo - ries _____

Copyright © 1991 by HAL LEONARD CORPORATION
International Copyright Secured   All Rights Reserved

heart _____ pre - pare _____ Him _____ room, _____ and heav'n and na - ture _____
floods, _____ rocks, hills _____ and _____ plains _____ Re - peat the sound - ing _____
make _____ His bless - ings _____ flow _____ Far as the curse is _____
of _____ His right - eous - ness _____ And won - ders of His _____

sing, _____ And _____ heav'n and na - ture _____ sing, _____ And _____
joy, _____ Re - peat the sound - ing _____ joy, _____ Re -
found, _____ Far _____ as the curse is _____ found, _____ Far _____
love, _____ And _____ won - ders of His _____ love, _____ And _____

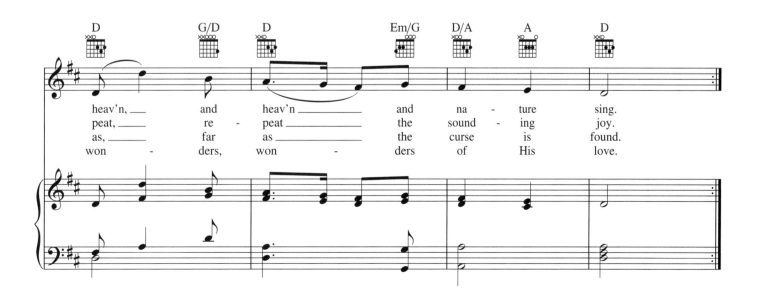

heav'n, _____ and heav'n _____ and na - ture sing.
peat, _____ re - peat _____ the sound - ing joy.
as, _____ far as _____ the curse is found.
won - ders, won - ders of His love.

Let It Snow! Let It Snow! Let It Snow!

Words by Sammy Cahn
Music by Jule Styne

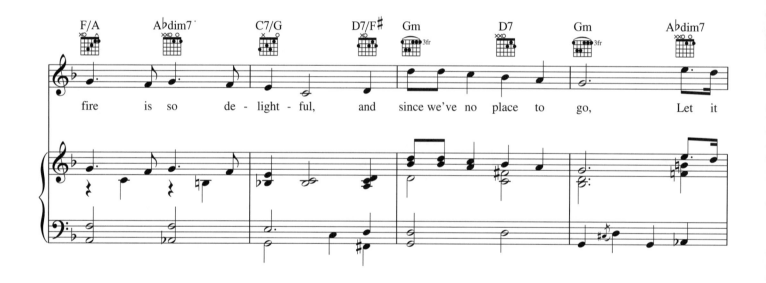

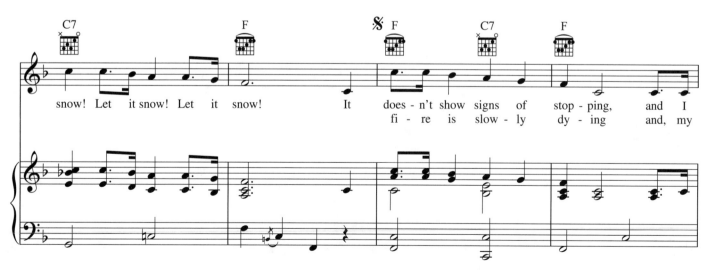

Copyright © 1945 by Producers Music Publishing Co., Inc. and Cahn Music Co.
Copyright Renewed
All Rights for Producers Music Publishing Co., Inc. Administered by Chappell & Co.
All Rights for Cahn Music Co. Administered by WB Music Corp.
International Copyright Secured   All Rights Reserved

Little Saint Nick

Words and Music by Brian Wilson and Mike Love

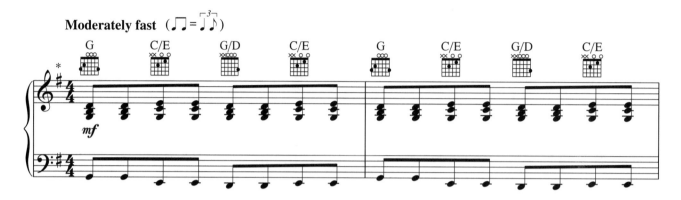

Ooh, Mer - ry Christ-mas, Saint Nick. Ooh. (Christ - mas comes this

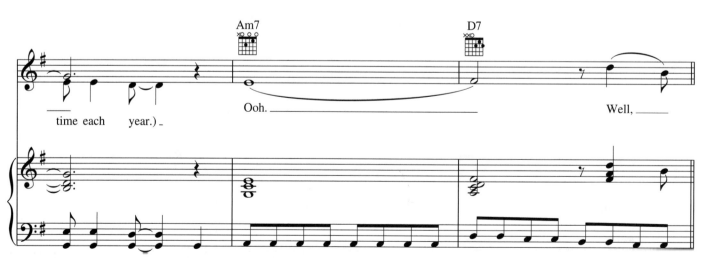

time each year.) Ooh. Well,

* Recorded a half step lower.

Copyright © 1963 IRVING MUSIC, INC.
Copyright Renewed
All Rights Reserved   Used by Permission

Mistletoe and Holly

Words and Music by Frank Sinatra, Dok Stanford and Henry W. Sanicola

Medium Bounce

Oh, by gosh, by gol - ly, it's time for mis - tle - toe and
Oh, by gosh, by jin - gle, it's time for car - ols and Kris
Oh, by gosh, by gol - ly, it's time for mis - tle - toe and

hol - ly, _____ tast - y pheas - ants, Christ - mas pres - ents,
Krin - gle, _____ o - ver - eat - ing, mer - ry greet - ings
hol - ly, _____ fan - cy ties an' gran - ny's pies an'

To Coda

coun - try-sides cov - ered with snow.
from _____ rel - a - tives you don't know.

Copyright © 1957 Barton Music Corp.
Copyright Renewed and Assigned to Sergeant Music Co. and Barton Music Corp.
All Rights on behalf of Sergeant Music Co. Administered by WB Music Corp.
All Rights Reserved   Used by Permission

The Most Wonderful Time of the Year

Words and Music by Eddie Pola and George Wyle

Copyright © 1963 Barnaby Music Corp.
Copyright Renewed 1991
International Copyright Secured   All Rights Reserved

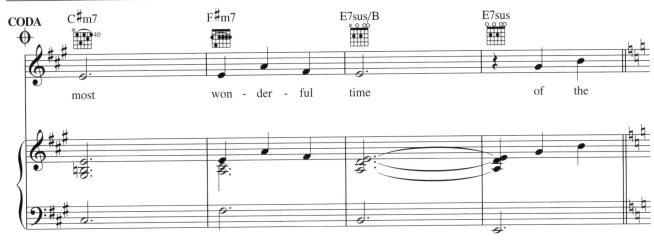

most won - der - ful time of the

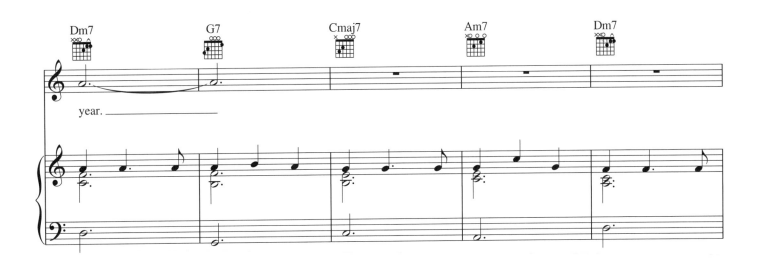

year. ___

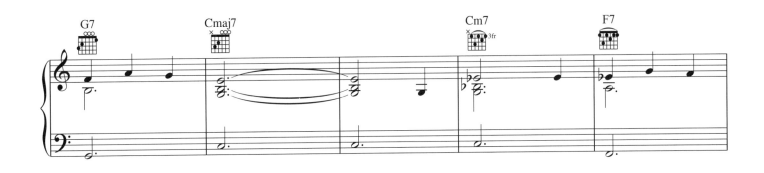

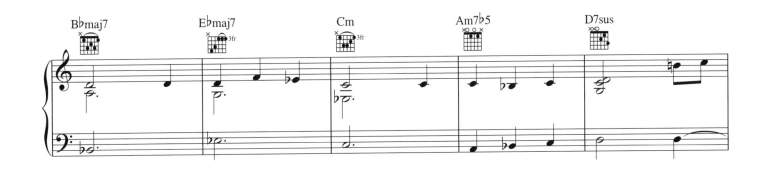

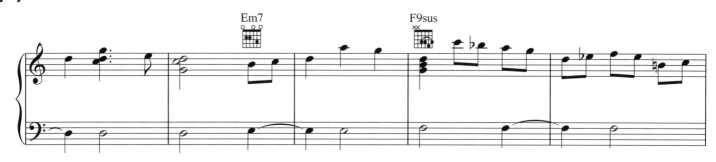

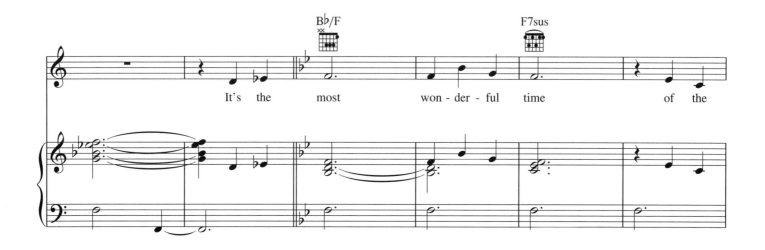

It's the most won-der-ful time of the

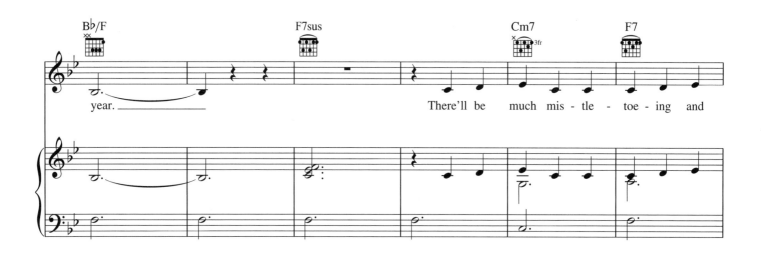

year. There'll be much mis-tle - toe-ing and

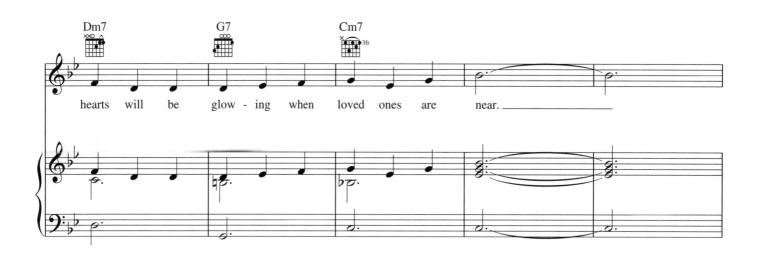

hearts will be glow-ing when loved ones are near.

My Favorite Things

from THE SOUND OF MUSIC
Lyrics by Oscar Hammerstein II
Music by Richard Rodgers

Copyright © 1959 by Richard Rodgers and Oscar Hammerstein II
Copyright Renewed
WILLIAMSON MUSIC owner of publication and allied rights throughout the world
International Copyright Secured   All Rights Reserved

O Christmas Tree

Traditional German Carol

Copyright © 1991 by HAL LEONARD CORPORATION
International Copyright Secured   All Rights Reserved

O Come, All Ye Faithful (Adeste Fideles)

Music by John Francis Wade
Latin Words translated by Frederick Oakeley

Copyright © 2003 by HAL LEONARD CORPORATION
International Copyright Secured   All Rights Reserved

O Holy Night

French Words by Placide Cappeau
English Words by John S. Dwight
Music by Adolphe Adam

Copyright © 1985 by HAL LEONARD CORPORATION
International Copyright Secured   All Rights Reserved

O Little Town of Bethlehem

Words by Phillips Brooks
Music by Lewis H. Redner

Copyright © 1982 by HAL LEONARD CORPORATION
International Copyright Secured   All Rights Reserved

Additional Lyrics

3. How silently, how silently
   The wondrous Gift is giv'n!
   So God imparts to human hearts
   The blessings of His heav'n.
   No ear may hear His coming,
   But in this world of sin,
   Where meek souls will receive Him still,
   The dear Christ enters in.

4. O Holy Child of Bethlehem,
   Descend to us, we pray.
   Cast out our sin, and enter in,
   Be born in us today.
   We hear the Christmas angels
   The great glad tidings tell.
   O come to us, abide with us,
   Our Lord Immanuel!

Rockin' Around the Christmas Tree

Music and Lyrics by Johnny Marks

Copyright © 1958 (Renewed 1986) St. Nicholas Music Inc., 1619 Broadway, New York, New York 10019
All Rights Reserved

Santa, Bring My Baby Back (To Me)

Words and Music by Claude DeMetruis and Aaron Schroeder

Copyright © 1957; Renewed 1985 Gladys Music (ASCAP) and Rachel's Own Music (ASCAP)
Worldwide Rights for Gladys Music Administered by Cherry Lane Music Publishing Company, Inc.
Worldwide Rights for Rachel's Own Music Administered by A. Schroeder International LLC
International Copyright Secured   All Rights Reserved

Rudolph the Red-Nosed Reindeer

Music and Lyrics by Johnny Marks

Copyright © 1949 (Renewed 1977) St. Nicholas Music Inc., 1619 Broadway, New York, New York 10019
All Rights Reserved

Santa Baby

By Joan Javits, Phil Springer and Tony Springer

© 1953 Trinity Music, Inc.
Copyright Renewed 1981 and Controlled in the U.S. by Philip Springer
Copyright Controlled for the world outside the U.S. by Alley Music Corp. and Trio Music Company
International Copyright Secured   All Rights Reserved

Santa Claus Is Comin' to Town

Words by Haven Gillespie
Music by J. Fred Coots

© 1934 (Renewed 1962) EMI FEIST CATALOG INC.
Rights for the Extended Renewal Term in the United States Controlled by HAVEN GILLESPIE MUSIC and EMI FEIST CATALOG INC.
All Rights for HAVEN GILLESPIE MUSIC Administered by THE SONGWRITERS GUILD OF AMERICA
All Rights outside the United States Controlled by EMI FEIST CATALOG INC. (Publishing) and ALFRED PUBLISHING CO., INC. (Print)
All Rights Reserved   Used by Permission

Shake Me I Rattle (Squeeze Me I Cry)

Words and Music by Hal Hackady and Charles Naylor

Copyright © 1957 (Renewed) by Regent Music Corporation (BMI)
International Copyright Secured   All Rights Reserved
Used by Permission

Silent Night

Words by Joseph Mohr, Translated by John F. Young
Music by Franz X. Gruber

Copyright © 1991 by HAL LEONARD CORPORATION
International Copyright Secured   All Rights Reserved

Silver Bells

from the Paramount Picture THE LEMON DROP KID
Words and Music by Jay Livingston and Ray Evans

Copyright © 1950 Sony/ATV Music Publishing LLC
Copyright Renewed
All Rights Administered by Sony/ATV Music Publishing LLC, 8 Music Square West, Nashville, TN 37203
International Copyright Secured All Rights Reserved

This Christmas

Words and Music by Donny Hathaway and Nadine McKinnor

(1.,4.) Hang   all the mis - tle - toe.__ I'm   gon - na get to know you bet - ter _____
(2.) Pres - ents and cards are here.__ My   world is filled with cheer and   you, _____
(3.) *Piano solo ad lib.*

Copyright © 1970 by Universal Music - MGB Songs, Kuumba Music Publishing and Crystal Raisin Music
Copyright Renewed
All Rights for Kuumba Music Publishing Administered by Universal Music - MGB Songs
International Copyright Secured   All Rights Reserved

The Twelve Days of Christmas

Traditional English Carol

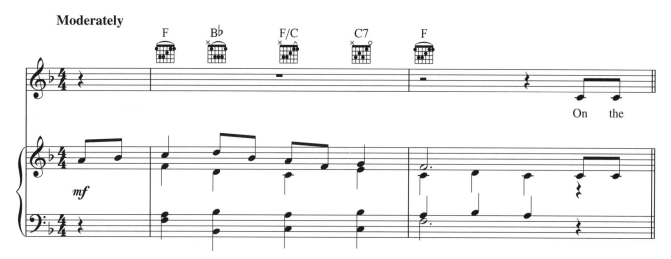

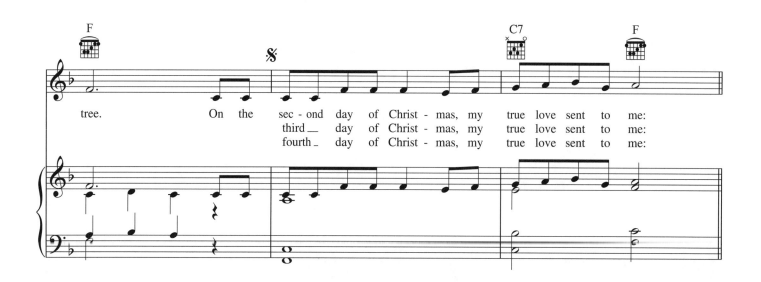

Copyright © 1991 by HAL LEONARD CORPORATION
International Copyright Secured   All Rights Reserved

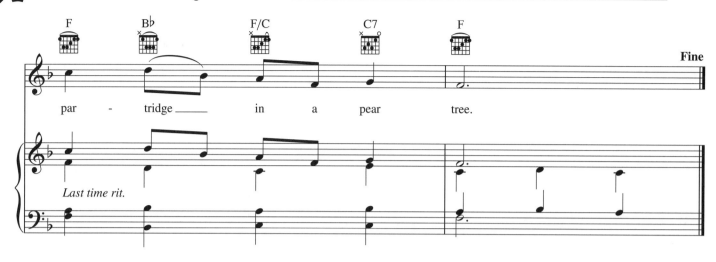

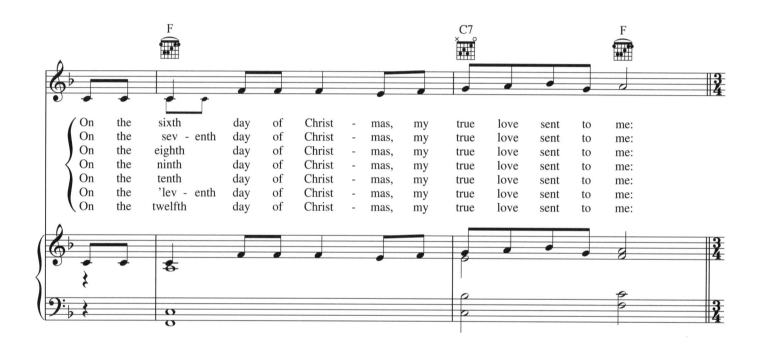

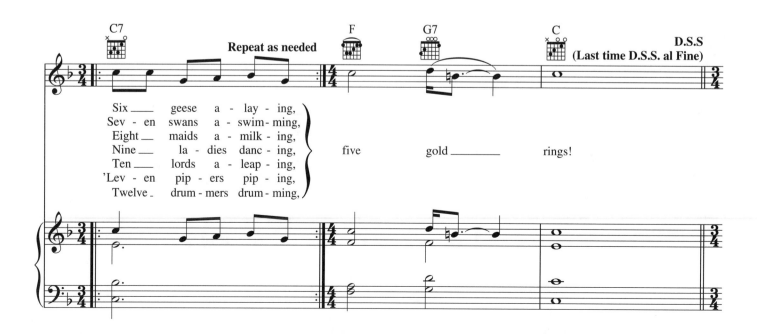

We Wish You a Merry Christmas

Traditional English Folksong

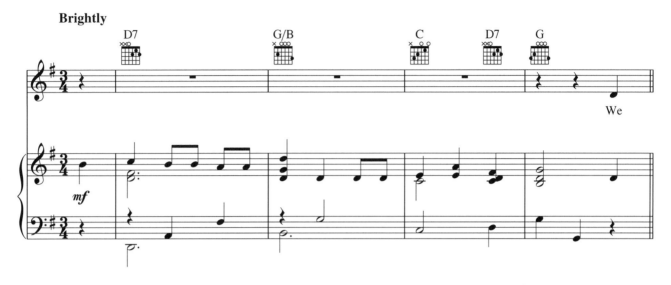

Copyright © 1993 by HAL LEONARD CORPORATION
International Copyright Secured   All Rights Reserved

What Are You Doing New Year's Eve?

By Frank Loesser

© 1947 (Renewed) FRANK MUSIC CORP.
All Rights Reserved

Wonderful Christmastime

Words and Music by Paul McCartney

© 1979 MPL COMMUNICATIONS LTD.
Administered by MPL COMMUNICATIONS, INC.
All Rights Reserved

You're All I Want for Christmas

Words and Music by Glen Moore and Seger Ellis

Copyright © 1948 SONGS OF UNIVERSAL, INC.
Copyright Renewed
All Rights Reserved   Used by Permission